Readiness for Ministry Through Spiritual Direction

by Forster Freeman

An Alban Institute Publication

Library of Congress Catalog Card Number 86-071059.

FOREWORD

Reuel Howe said many clergy "were successful people who were wearing themselves out being a success just because of what was missing inside." The lack of any attention to spiritual formation Roy Oswald noted in the training of 102 recent seminary graduates was also the experience of Forster Freeman, Minister of Spiritual Training, First Congregational Church of Berkeley, CA. Looking back at his seminary training, Freeman remembered that "the spiritual guidance I hoped to provide to parishioners I not only was not being trained to give but also had not experienced myself."

Reflecting on his own and others' experience of being <u>unready</u> for ministry, Freeman decided to carry out research to test the hypothesis that clergy will be better prepared to enter into effective ministries if they have had specific assistance with their personal spiritual formation. To academic and practical preparation Freeman added weekly spiritual direction sessions with ten students at Harvard and Andover Newton during an entire academic year. Through four full case studies the reader can join him as he journeyed with three women and one man through months of struggle and discovery. Freeman describes his role as that of a "midwife," "fostering a person's own discovery of the divine grace and will."

The results of this spiritual journey with four students are intriguing. One student concluded that "the effect of the spiritual direction experience has been to make me more <u>attentive</u>" to course work, conversations with others, and field education. Freeman analyzes similiarities and differences in the students' experience and use of direction. The uniqueness of each student's struggle stands out. And there are common themes as well. The students resisted the intimacy with God for which they yearned, sensing the risk of being led where they would not choose to go. Their awareness of their own resistance should be one useful tool in future ministry. Several were surprised by improved relationships with other people. Freeman concludes the study with specific recommendations for seminarians and judicatories.

The importance of this book extends to clergy who now hunger for the help in spiritual formation they did not receive in seminary. Listening in on Freeman's case studies will also be useful to the general reader who senses a spiritual hunger that is not being assuaged, most particularly in liberal Protestant churches. And it is a must for anyone involved in sponsoring or educating candidates for ministry and for all those who support spiritual leaders in their vocations.

Celia Allison Hahn
Director of Publications
The Alban Institute, Inc.

TABLE OF CONTENTS

ACKNOWLEDGMENTS

God has repeatedly astonished me by generously
providing all the people and arrangments needed since
first guiding me toward the studies and experiences
leading up to this publication.

The people most directly involved with my research
were the teachers in the Joint Program in Spiritual
Direction who also provided invaluable help as
members of my Project Committee. They are the
Director, Anne Harvey, S.N.D., and the two Readers,
William A. Barry, S.J. and Brian O. McDermott, S.J.

The other very significant faculty contributors to
my progress were my Supervisor, Madeline Birmingham,
r.c., and my own spiritual director, William J.
Connolly, S.J. The spiritual directees with whom I
worked aided my project far beyond their knowing. I
am grateful to the administrations of Harvard
Divinity School and Andover Newton Theological School
for permission and referrals to work with students.

I am very grateful to Celia Allison Hahn, The
Alban Institute's Director of Publications. Others
who read the manuscript and provided valuable
comments are: Loren B. Mead, Roy M. Oswald, Tilden
H. Edwards, Jr., Elaine Norton Hooker, Dorothy
Gheith. The typist was Robin Turnbaugh.

To all I give my thanks.

Affirming me throughout these studies and my whole
journey is my closest spiritual companion and life
partner, Julia. To her, and to our Master Teacher,
Jesus, I am most thankful of all.

"It was then that, filled with joy by
the Holy Spirit, he said, ˹I bless you,
Father, Lord of heaven and earth, for
hiding these things from the learned
and clever and revealing them to mere
children.˺"

> Luke 10:21 (Jerusalem Bible)

"For the Church cannot change into
something or other at will, arbitrar-
ily, but only into a new presence of
its old reality, into the presence and
future of its past, of the Gospel, of
the grace and truth of God himself."

> Karl Rahner
> The Christian of the Future
> p. 36

PREFACE

The evolution of this monograph is inseparably part
of my personal pilgrimage.

In the moments when I have been most clear in
self-understanding, it has become obvious that the
central issue in my life has been that of being in
such direct relationship with the Creator who
designed and redeemed me that I would discover God´s
purpose for me, and actualize that plan and the
divinity within my nature in a way that would bring
blessing to others. I engaged in prayer in my youth
and much of my adulthood in a comparatively primitive
and tentative fashion. It became evident to me that
most people who pray do it for communication mostly
from their own side. In spite of numerous familiar
suggestions that God answers prayers, relatively few
have been taught how to hear the answers, and in fact
have some doubt about whether they are capable enough
or worthy enough for such privileged dialogue.

Have the impediments we erect against free speaking and hearing ever been thus? In the seventeenth
century, Madame Jeanne Guyon addressed our situation:

I realize that the prospect of living a "life of
piety" is frightening to most Christians! And
prayer is viewed as a very difficult attainment.
Consequently, most believers are too discouraged
at the very outset even to take the first step in
this direction. It is true that if you consider
the difficulty of some new undertaking it can
surely cause you to despair and make you relectant
to begin. On the other hand, the desirableness of
such an adventure—and the idea that it may easily
be accomplished—can cause you to launch out with
vigor....

We need only a little courage and perseverence.
Actually, we have enough of both in our earthly
affairs, but none at all in the only thing that
really matters. (Luke 10:42)[1]

In due time, three decades into my career, God
finally made it clear to me that I was to engage in
graduate studies toward certification and a Doctor of
Ministry in Spiritual Direction. In the course of
conducting my research project and writing my doc-
toral thesis, I became strongly convinced that I
needed to share my learnings so that other church
leaders could profit from them with me.
The question with which I have dealt in the
research is: "Is the contemplative approach to
spiritual direction an effective way to advance
Protestants' readiness for Christian ministry?" I
have had in mind not only seminarians and ordained
clergy, but all active church people as being personally engaged in ministries. I have given specific
attention to Protestants because of my own affilia-
tion with the Presbyterian Church (U.S.A.) and the
United Church of Christ, and also because I have
perceived that the Roman Catholic tradition within
which I was pursuing my graduate studies had been
more faithful in providing spiritual guidance and so
had much to teach us.
Ever since I was doing my M.Div. studies in three
seminaries and received almost no help with my personal spiritual development, I have carried an urgent
concern that Protestant seminarians should have such
assistance provided to them. I believe that this is
as essential as academic studies in preparation for

their eventually giving guidance to others in ministry, and for action to bring sanity and peace and community to our world.

I did my first year of studies at Harvard Divinity School and the Swedenborg School of Theology, my second and third years at Union Theological Seminary in New York City. By the time I was in my middler year I perceived that the spiritual guidance I hoped to provide eventually to parishioners I not only was not being trained to give but also had not experienced myself. How would I be able to provide what I had not received? There must be some approaches, such as devotional practices, that would help to develop maturity in the faith, I thought, but no one had ever instructed me or given specific encouragement in that direction. I was receiving superb instruction from theological and ethical giants concerning what people thought about God and Jesus Christ, church operation and Christian engagement with society, but scarcely a word on the possibility of knowing God personally and responding in an increasingly intimate and empowering relationship.

Reading the New Testament encouraged me to suppose that such a relationship had once been available and necessary to the church's vitality, and possibly still was. Having been brought up on the seer, Emanuel Swedenborg, and having read about experiences of other saints further encouraged me to believe that personal communication was still transpiring in the lives of at least a few, and that God's desire might be for a great deal more such attention and participation on our parts.

What I needed, in my uncertainty and inarticulateness, was for a seminary to take initiative not only to make formal provision for a spiritual direction program to complement the intellectual curriculum and the practicums, but also to incorporate it into the catalogue and orientation sessions, and openly to encourage voluntary participation. My seminaries, like other Protestant schools in those days, however, saw their educational responsibility to be in the realm of cognitive study and field work. The spiritual development was expected somehow to come naturally.

Throughout the thirty-five years since my ordination I have held a strong concern that Protestant seminarians should have provided to them the spiritual assistance that I found lacking, and that pastors should be equipped to provide it for their parishioners. This passion has led me in recent years to attend training sessions in spiritual guidance given by Jack Biersdorf, Andrew Canale, Tilden Edwards, Morton Kelsey, and the Holy Order of MANS. I became increasingly conscious of the spiritual direction practice and training offered in the Roman Catholic and Orthodox traditions, even though in their institutions, too, there has developed some division between the monastic and the scholastic. I learned that it was common for there to be full-time formation teams provided to students in Roman Catholic seminaries, together with courses on the history of spirituality and on spiritual theology, to help integrate academic and field education and spiritual training. I thought that some Protestants ought to be trained to do such work. In time, through a sequence of unmistakable signals, I acknowledged that God was guiding me to be one such person.

After investigating both Protestant and Roman Catholic training centers for spiritual guidance in the United States, I could see that the best one for me was the Joint Program in Spiritual Direction. This Program was provided for a few years by the Weston School of Theology and the Center for Religious Development, both Jesuit institutions in Cambridge, Massachusetts. I was abundantly blessed during the year of training for certification as a spiritual director and the additional year for my D.Min. research project on which this writing is based.

CHAPTER I

An Urgent Need in Protestantism

The History of Christian Spiritual Guidance[1]

Spiritual direction is a ministry that has been practiced in the Christian Church since its early centuries. Some of the Desert Fathers described their practices in writing as including preaching, mutual direction by members of the community, individual meetings with spiritual mothers or fathers, and letters of direction given by bishops and other leaders, all undergirded by examples from the Scripture and other stories of the saints. This tradition developed through the Medieval period to a distinct flowering in the sixteenth and seventeenth centuries, particularly focused in the publication of the Spiritual Exercises of St. Ignatius, which was systematically based on Scripture, the life of Christ, and well tested dynamics of the inner process of dialoguing with them.

Professor Ephrem Carr estimates that more than ninety percent of present-day Roman Catholic training programs in spiritual direction in the United States are under the auspices of the Society of Jesus, which was founded in the sixteenth century by St. Ignatius of Loyola. Two other highly influential figures of that same era, St. Teresa of Avila and St. John of the Cross, promulgated their conviction that spiritual direction for both people under vows and lay church members was a necessity for the renewal of the church.

The practice of individual spiritual direction nearly disappeared among Roman Catholics during the last couple of centuries, partly due to some directors' arrogating power to themselves, to theological controversies about the movement of grace, and to Jansenism's rigidity and negative view of human nature. It has been only as recently as the Second Vatican Council that this ministry has been

revived and that women as well as men have been
trained to offer it. Up until the late 1960s, what
was called spiritual direction in this century
generally consisted of pastoral counseling dealing
with problems rather than assisting people with their
relationships with God. Questions about prayer
usually had to do with whether or not a person was
fulfilling the obligation to say prayers rather than
with whether the prayers were effecting a lively
dialogic connection and a direct influence on active
living.

The Protestant reformers provided extensive
"direction of conscience" to their followers, more
often through letters than in person. This was
notably true of Martin Luther, Martin Bucer and John
Calvin. Some others, abhorring Roman practices and
fearful of clericalism, rejected such individual
counsel while emphasizing the priesthood of all
believers. An abundance of examples of one-to-one
continuing guidance are to be found among the
Puritans, even though some like John Bunyan
vigorously opposed such interchanges in favor of
solitary individual pursuits. Mutual direction has
been common historically among Quakers, in Methodist
bands and class meetings, and in Presbyterian zone
meetings gathered preceding the observance of the
Lord's Supper. In our century, personal direction
was important to Dietrich Bonhoeffer, while its worth
was denied by Karl Barth.

Unbalanced Training in Contemporary Schools

It has been almost unheard of until very recently for
Protestant seminaries, especially the theologically
more liberal seminaries, to offer their students
ongoing personal guidance specifically for their
spiritual formation. The naming of so many such
institutions as "theological seminaries" has proved
to be a self-fulfilling prophecy. they set
themselves about the intellectual task of doing
theology systematically, logically, creatively,
relevantly. Other disciplines like Bible, history,
ethics, Christian education and homiletics often came
to be regarded as clustered around, and in the
service of, theology.

It was easily forgotten that the true origin of accurate theology, having to do with God and the relations between God and creation, was necessarily not in brilliant speculation but in actual revelatory experiences that had as much to do with heart as with head. It is little wonder that, in those schools where left brain cognitive processes came to be proudly swollen into dominance at the expense of the affective possibilities, some people were wont to observe that "the word of the Lord was rare in those days; there was no frequent vision."[2] By some strange perversity, entire denominations seemed to become fixated on the predominant ascendency of the mind in religion, losing sight of Jesus' number one emphasis, "The Lord our God, the Lord is one; and you shall love the Lord your God with all your heart, and with all your soul, and with all your mind, and with all your strength."[3]

One symptom of such a condition is suggested in the claim of one journal that,

In a recent survey of one of the large well-known theological colleges here in the United States, ninety-three percent of the students studying for the ministry said "I have no devotional life." They will become powerless preachers. They may be able to develop a strong, pleasing personality and become elegant orators, but they will never be able to communicate God's message to man because communication is supernatural (the work of the Holy Spirit) and the Spirit only comes to us in power through fervent heartfelt prayer and communication with God.[4]

A study by the Metropolitan Ecumenical Training Center came at this phenomenon from a different direction. It included interviews with an ecumenically representative group of congregational members whose pastors had selected them as being most spiritually mature. One of the findings was:

Religious experience by many was spoken of in terms of answers to prayer, and sometimes the gift of faith. In the majority of these cases God was perceived in very personal, intimate terms, and as

being responsive to their needs. The personalness
and directness of relationship tended to decline
in direct proportion to the quantity of liberal
arts and theological (as opposed to Biblical)
education.[5]

Reuel Howe added this observation from his experience, when speaking of awakening men and women to the
meaning of being, and of working with clergy after
founding the Institute for Advanced Pastoral Studies
in 1957:

Many of them were even afraid of having allowed
themselves to get into the ministry and realized
afterward that something was missing inside and
they had only the outside stuff with which to
carry on. We were Christian ministers and the
Holy Spirit was supposed to be incarnate in us. .
. . That was what was missing. . . .many of
these people were surprising, because they were
successful people who were wearing themselves out
being a success just because of what was missing
inside.[6]

An Alban Institute research team recently surveyed
102 graduates of ten different Protestant seminaries,
representing eight different denominations, who had
been engaged in parish ministry for one to three
years. These clergy said:

The greatest difficulty I seem to be having is
being aware of my own spirituality. I don't seem
to have enough resources of faith to draw on in
this vocation. I don't seem to have adequate
spiritual disciplines that continually nourish
that faith. My prayer and worship life does not
seem to feed my own needs in this situation.[7]

The report on the survey provides this distressing
further elucidation:

Sustaining and fostering personal integration and
wholeness within a parish setting was a difficult
task for these graduates. Many found themselves
disillusioned by their failure to maintain their
own sense of spiritual feeding and growth. Most
were genuinely surprised as they had assumed that

their spiritual life would be easily maintained or
even grow by virtue of their work as pastors.
Instead, they experienced a gradual decline or
loss of spiritual awareness and wholeness during
the two years following graduation. . . .

Only in retrospect did they realize that they had
gone through four years of seminary education
without once being asked about their personal
life, their personal relationship with God, their
experiences of Christ, the meaning of suffering in
their lives, the ups and downs of their own spiritual journey, the ways in which they got centered
and grounded, their personal discipline of meditation, prayer, and scriptural study, the spiritual
giants of their lives and their attempts at finding a spiritual father/mother/guru/friend for the
present, and the activities that fed them spiritually.[8]

Tilden Edwards and a team who studied the situation among seminaries in 1979 and 1980 drew these
conclusions:

1. No long-term process of spiritual formation
can be assumed in the background of entering
students, and perhaps for a number of faculty as
well. . . .

2. Individual conscience has become increasingly
important in a context of few or no agreed-upon
norms. Students are pressed toward a desire for
more ongoing personal spiritual guidance to help
them discern the way the Spirit is moving in their
particular situation and to help with the development and accountability for a disciplined attentiveness to this grace, individually and corpor-
ately.

As this need has grown, there appears to be a
shortage of faculty/staff persons who feel competence, confidence, and call to be such guides.[9]

Meanwhile, most church members have no notion of
the spiritual dryness of the typical seminary scene.

Those to whom I have described contemporary training have been amazed and shocked, since they had all along assumed that spiritual preparation was the primary ingredient in training for ordination. They continued to be frustrated in their expectations that seminary graduates would be spiritual guides.

In keeping with this, the Readiness for Ministry Project team of the Association of Theological Schools concluded from its research,

> A closer scrutiny reveals the continuing request of the community of faith that their leaders be more than persons who have learned facts and mastered techniques. First, the community demands that they be persons who have experienced the reality of being freed by the Gospel, who have personally glimpsed meaning in the midst of a fractured world. . . .
>
> The language of the Bible reflects the distinction between "knowing about" and "knowing experientially."[10]

It is not difficult to comprehend the forces that drew church educators toward an almost exclusively cognitive approach to the sublime. Part of it was in the "cultural trance"[11] of our secular, scientific, rational mind which seduced religionists into wanting to be accepted and accredited in terms of what was valued by the pedestaled and powerful intelligentsia. Part of it was a continuing suspicion of, and prejudice against, Roman Catholic practices, or what were thought to be such. Hence, a person must work out a private spirituality, if desired, by faith and grace, and not rely on any priestly intermediary-intruder. There was also a fear in liberal, mainline Protestant circles of risking pietistic and moralistic values, anti-intellectualism, naive and irresponsible "mystical" escapism, and passive-dependent relationships. And there was a naive assumption that inner development would be adequately nurtured by the unexamined customary seminary practices. Hence, as recently as 1983 a respected seminary president, describing "the anatomy of an accredited seminary as a graduate school of higher education," did include

the spiritual element in a list of six ingredients.
But the only helps he prescribed were the meager
"opportunities for the spiritual formation of
candidates through chapel worship, study and
play."[12]

A frequent response from seminary faculty and
staff members, when the idea is suggested of making
spiritual guides available to students, is: "I see
no need at all for such an addition. After all, most
of us are ordained and have had some experience in
counseling, and the students know that most of us
willingly make ourselves available to them if they
want to talk privately about something that´s on
their minds." Such a response reveals a lack of
comprehension either of the students´ needs or of the
nature of spiritual direction. It also fails to take
into account that faculty and staff members have
rarely been trained to be ministers of spiritual
direction or received such guidance themselves, and
that the students generally do not feel freedom to
disclose themselves intimately to a person who
exercises the authority to assign academic grades and
make evaluations for future advancement, even though
there are some notable exceptions.

In a few cases, faculty resistance even becomes
defensive, so as to produce convoluted logic, as is
represented by a professor of the Church of Scotland. Hugh Anderson made reference in an article to
"two leading proposals made lately in Scotland for
the improvement and enhancement of theological
education."

> The second proposal is that in Scotland theologi-
> cal education has been for too long strictly
> academic and that much more time and energy ought
> to be spent in assisting students in the spiritual
> life, in prayer and devotion. . . .

> As to the second proposal mentioned above, no one,
> I suppose, would care to deny for a moment that
> spirituality, prayer and devotion are absolutely
> vital to the minister´s life and work. Neverthe-
> less to separate spirituality amost entirely from
> the intellectual or academic pursuit is to take a
> much too atomistic view of the preparation of

the total self for ministry. The disciplining of
the mind and prayer and devotion seem to be insep-
arable. . . . (What I have called the atomistic
view) carries with it the gravest risk of all, of
encouraging the further spread of anti-intellectualism in the churches.[13]

It is little wonder that the reticence to take
students' spiritual needs seriously has resulted in
disillusionment of some students and of many more
seminary graduates who have felt stunted in their
growth and seriously inadequate for providing effective ministry. The situation has in some places been
serious enough to have motivated the Danish novelist,
Johannes Anker-Larsen, to write:

I was young, and the world was beautiful, but I
kept looking for a sunrise which was to make
everything more alive.

I looked for it in the theological faculty. To a
thirsting soul, this is like a desert. It re-
minded me of a time during the war, when one day I
entered a cafe where I hoped to get a cup of coffee, and got something which was called coffee and
looked like coffee, but wasn't.[14]

An Increasingly Conscious Hunger

Fortunately, rejection of concerted attention to
spiritual formation is not universal. On the contrary, students and other church members have long
been crying for help in this area, and the last
decade has brought a rising tide of favorable concern
among their teachers. A Task Force of Spiritual
Development, formed by the Association of Theological
Schools, published a report on the findings of its
research in this field in 1972. Although the Task
Force report displays little awareness that there is
a tradition of trained spiritual directors, it does
document the beginning of the rising awareness. The
report quotes Charles Fielding's statement, "A professor's most important contribution to professional
formation is constituted by what in general he is
seen to do rather than by the information he con-
veys." It continues with its own observations:

12

[Although commitment to Christ cannot be assumed
to be the motivation of some students,] many
others are honestly, diligently, even desperately
searching for the pearl. They may have come with
the mistaken notion that "knowledge about" is
equivalent to, or will inevitably result in,
"knowledge of." Surely, however, no seminary
faculty would confuse knowledge of the box with
the experience of holding the pearl in one's own
hands. . . .

The spiritual formation and development of seminary students begins with, and is dependent upon,
the spiritual formation and development of the
faculty.

The implications of this statement are as threatening as they are promising, as frightening as they
are exciting.[15]

In a more recent follow-up on the 1972 report, the
Association of Theological Schools and the Shalem
Institute on Spirituality conducted a joint project
dealing with the expanding interest in the spiritual
formation of both students and faculty. Each school
was invited to send a team of people to one of six
regional conferences held in the United States in
1979 and 1980. Each participant was invited to read
in advance three short background papers and to complete a questionnaire. The findings from these
conferences and other parts of the project were published in Theological Education, the semiannual
journal of the A.T.S.
 The questions and the pattern of responses reveal
the continuing concerns and needs of faculty:

1. What is the most important concern you bring
to this conference regarding spiritual formation?
Two areas of concern are evident. First there is
a very personal concern about how to develop,
model, and offer personal help for the spiritual
life. How may I better understand and develop a
disciplined prayer life? How can I be helpful to
students in their unique personal spiritual
development? What kind of preparation do I need

to offer such help? Am I meant to do it? How do
I overcome the evaluation barrier with students?
. . .

2. Has your school developed an intentional,
mutually explored set of assumptions and practices
in this area? Most faculty answer this with a
qualified or unqualified "no." Most of the exceptions are from Roman Catholic schools, though even
some of these think that they have no really
clear, consciously intentional, mutually explored
process. . . .

Some schools traditionally regard the religious
communities and churches to which seminarians
belong as the appropriate base for spiritual
formation.[16]

Such encouraging evidence of awakening concern is
one of numerous streams feeding into a strongly increasing current. The following is a brief sampling
from such streams. One example was seen in 1967,
when Arnold B. Come delivered his inaugural address
upon becoming president of San Francisco Theological
Seminary. He stated:

I intend, for one, to do all in my power to
attract to this place those young men and women
who have the courage and the imagination to open
themselves to the leading of God's spirit, to do
everything necessary to give them that atmosphere
and environment that will encourage them on the
way of this adventure. . . . So this board has
helped to gather a faculty that is brilliantly
equipped and ready to guide those young men and
women in this adventure of spiritual discovery.[17]

Two years later, Richard Shaull, of Princeton
Theological Seminary, wrote:

This suggests that the starting point for theological reflection today is not the development of
a new conceptual framework, but the lived experience of a new reality. And if we take the
biblical story seriously, this reality is of a

14

very specific type: the experience of freedom,
grace and joy, and the emergence of new life
styles, which come to us in the midst of our
exodus and exile from contemporary forms of
bondage and oppression. . . .

Unfortunately, most education. . .is still
dominated by old teaching methods that stress the
passing on of knowledge and information from the
one who teaches to the one who is taught, and thus
focuses more on the program of study than on the
needs and interests of the student.[18]

Amos N. Wilder, a professor emeritus at Harvard
Divinity School, added in 1973:

My plea for a theopoetic means doing more justice
to the role of the symbolic and the prerational in
the way we deal with experience. We should recognize that human nature and human societies are
more deeply motivated by images and mythologies
than by ideas. This is where power lies and where
the future is shaped. . . . Any deep renewal of
language or rebirth of images arises from within
and from beyond our control. Nevertheless, we can
help prepare the event, both by moral and spiritual discipline and by attention to the modes and
vehicles of the Word. . .many evidences in our
culture of a turn toward what we can speak of
loosely as the mystical, the prerational and the
imaginative.[19]

By 1976, the Pacific School of Regligion appointed
a Task Force on Religious Formation, "to explore what
meaning spirituality has in a pluralistic inter-
denominational seminary community." The Task Force
conducted interviews of several hours each with 51
"faculty, alumni, students, prospective students and
drop-outs."

From the depth interviews we were able to identify
five strands (or salient themes):
    (1) Spirituality as personal growth toward
wholeness;
    (2) Spirituality as relationship to the
Ultimate;

(3)   Spirituality as associated with religious
practice;
(4)   Spirituality as social concern; and
(5)   Spirituality as mystical experience.[20]

Along with such utterances from faculty members
and task forces, students on campuses across the
country have been becoming increasingly conscious and
articulate and pleading about their needs for
spiritual mentors. Here are just three examples.
The first is from the 1981 President's Report, by
Donald W. Shriver, Jr., of Union Theological
Seminary, in New York City:

Martin Buber said, "It is not instruction which
educates; it is the teacher who educates." A few
years ago a member of our faculty said to me,
"Early in my teaching career at Union I dwelt
almost exclusively in my classes on the academic
materials of my field. Lately, however, I have
noticed that students seem to be very curious
about the faith-commitments of faculty. They seem
especially grateful for an occasional word about
the reasons for a teacher's devotion to the
Christian faith, the church, and the profession of
teaching. Our students' need for such testimony
seems to have grown over the past few years
. . . ."

In 1964 a member of the student body put down this
plea to the faculty: "All of us have very
personal questions which must be answered, and are
anxiously wrestling with our faith (or lack of
it). This is largely the basis of our unrest.
This restlessness cannot be solved by rearranging
schedules and revision of the order in which we
study Niebuhr, Tillich, and vonRad. Rather, I
want simply (and profoundly) to know (all logical
proofs and problems aside) why the men who are
teaching me have decided to give their life to
this! And this I must know if I am to remain in
seminary."[21]

Also in 1981, as a result of a widespread ferment
among the students at Andover Newton Theological
School, members of the Women's Caucus there

circulated a questionnaire to both Protestant and
Roman Catholic students. Part of what the 93
Protestants replied was:

"I. Some assumptions we've heard. . .are they
     true or false for you?
     5. There is a pastoral counseling program
     here which meets students' needs."
Responses: True 5; False 51; ? 32.

IV. Of the following, rank, in order of
preference, who you would seek out in time of
need."
     The tally of those designated as priorities
     1-4 was:
     Chaplain 63
     Pastoral Counselor 59
     Spiritual Director 52
     Psychological Counselor 18
     Dean of Students 17

Some of the comments that students added at the
end of the questionnaire were:

"We need a pastor's pastor here--or a system for
helping each other."

"Would like to have access to spiritual director
on this campus and/or chaplain."

"Would have sought out a counselor at ANTS if it
were easily available, cheap or free, and if I
didn't think counselors here would be biased in a
narrow parochial Protestant ethic sense."

"There is a need for students to have a
professional person on this campus who cares and
has TIME to help with spiritual direction and/or
other personal problems!"

"Now we have no place to go for spiritual
needs."[22]

The Andover Newton administration by the next
year, in acknowledgment of changing student
awareness, inaugurated a volunteer chaplaincy

program. The guiding committee for this program also launched a trial Saturday workshop, as the student entered campus for the fall of 1983, entitled, "On the Spiritual Life—Don't Leave Andover Newton Without One." Although many supposed that this program would do well to attract a dozen women and men, 50 attended.

Henri Nouwen, in his second year of teaching at Harvard, offered for the spring term of 1984 a course, Introduction to the Christian Spiritual Life. Two hundred-thirty students enrolled. He had to use a lottery for enrollment in his limited-number more intensive course in spirituality. These two courses are in addition to a third already taught by Krister Stendahl.

Movements of restlessness, reassessment and testing of the possibilities are noticeable at seminaries in widespread regions. In the estimates of many, God is gradually enticing us away from secure-feeling old patterns that will not suffice for a new day, providing hints of vistas of which we were not capable of conceiving in earlier decades.

The human heart can go to the lengths of God.
Dark and cold we may be, but this
Is no winter now. The frozen misery
Of centuries breaks, cracks, begins to move,
The thunder is the thunder of the floes,
The thaw, the flood, the upstart Spring. . . .
Affairs are now soul size.
The enterprise
Is exploration into God,
Where no nation's foot has ever trodden yet. . . .
Where are you going? It takes
So many thousand years to wake,
But will you wake for pity's sake. . . .[23]

CHAPTER II

Increasing Readiness for Ministry by Providing Spiritual Direction

The Hypothesis of this Research

Within the context of my fervent concern for the spiritual hungers of church members and clergy, I chose for my research sample some seminary students in two institutions who were interested in having a spiritual guide.

The ruling hypothesis during my research was that men and women students in Protestant seminaries will benefit more from their training for service in the church and world when that training includes specific assistance with their personal spiritual formation. This hypothesis is rooted in the Scriptural paradigm of transformation for effectiveness, of becoming fully alive and awake human beings in Christ in order to be most keenly useful in the service of the Servant Master.[1]

Part of the goal of a seminary must be to assist each student with spiritual formation, toward the realization of her/his (and the neighbor's) true self, God's image individualized. Such realization is simultaneous--almost synonymous--with experiencing personal communication with God. It is to become open and available to the moving of the Spirit of the Christ, the divine power that frees us from our biases, ambitions, defenses, guilts, anxieties, lethargies, alienations, ego-centeredness. It is kenosis, crucifixion of the false self, abandonment to grace, flowing with providence. It is to be entered by eternal life while still dwelling on this material plane. It is to welcome such a completely transforming take-over that one's awareness is sometimes called Christ consciousness, or living as a new being in Christ, or being one with the Father, or return home to the banquet, or the New Jerusalem. One manifests gifts and fruits of the Spirit, and one's actions come at least occasionally to be recognized as the Master's actions. It is reconciliation with God, self, others and society—leading eventually even to reconciliation of organized power systems. Such transformation is suggested in numerous New Covenant declarations, such as: the person "who has faith in me will do what I am doing; and. . .will do greater things still"; and "let your minds be remade and your whole nature thus transformed. Then you will be able to discern the will of God, and to know what is good, acceptable and perfect"; and "in fact the kingdom of God is among (or within) you."[2]

Although such transformation is a lifetime process rather than a requisite for the granting of an M.Div., it is feasible to provide specific aid to students who are interested in moving steadily on the journey. A seminary that is intellectually rigorous and that, rather than reducing the spiritual to the theological and academic, takes responsibility for providing vitally for its students' spiritual development, meets their needs far more completely, treats them holistically as persons, and manifests its own Christian integrity. There are recently clear signs of hope that our schools are discovering the synthesis that is essential for the becoming processes of their potential ministers and the people they are to serve.

Spiritual formation in the case of most seminarians is focused toward the specific vocational goal of Christian ministry. I understand Christian ministry to be the service to God and others that is given by people who are conscious of being disciples of Jesus Christ and empowered by His Spirit, whether they are ordained, vowed or lay persons, and whether or not they are employed by a part of the institutional Christian Church.

The focus for my research was narrowed particularly to students' readiness for ministry. A way I had of defining what this means was to consult the two volume monograph, Readiness for Ministry, published in 1975-76 by the Readiness for Ministry Project team of the Association of Theological Schools. The A.T.S. has 196 member schools. The project, begun in 1973, involved 4,895 representatives of forty-seven denominations in one's rating the importance of criteria for readiness, in response to a pervasive sense of need among educators and church leaders. It was learned that denominational leaders

> find that the questions a congregation raises about a potential minister do not concern the number of courses completed but revolve about such areas as wisdom and knowledge, pastoral skills, psychological maturity, and the strength of faith.[3]

The project team concluded that the quality of seminary education "can be assessed best by determining the degree to which those who experience such education are indeed prepared for the practice of ministry."[4]

The team identified 444 criterion statements, then formed these into sixty-four clusters, from which they arrived at the ten major characteristics that both clergy and lay members across denominational lines agreed were most valued in clergy, plus criteria arrived at through second-order factor analysis of the clusters. Section V, on The Minister´s Personal Commitment of Faith, is relevant to my research. The four criteria within it that were strongly chosen by both clergy and lay respondents were: service without regard for acclaim, Christian example, acknowledgment of limitations and religious commitment.[5]

The other area which I recognized would be the most likely to be directly affected through spiritual direction is Factor 2. It

> describes ministry as it relates specifically to spiritual needs. The highest loading cluster includes statements such as "Shows sensitivity to the leading of the holy Spirit," and "Holds that in the midst of serious problems, God is at work. . . ." There is an emphasis on personal morality and conduct, and a willingness to pray for and with others. This factor seems to emphasize the more transcendental, spiritual domain of ministry.[6]

These are some definitions of the marks of
readiness to perform Christian ministry.
There are several possible avenues that lie before
seminaries to be explored for facilitating spiritual
growth along with the academic. Some are courses,
such as in spiritual theology, which can describe a
theoretical and interdisciplinary foundation for the
spiritual life, and in the history of spirituality.
It is indispensable to add to such cognitive studies
an unaccustomed emphasis on the experiential and
affective domain, on the practice of personal
disciplines and interpersonal exchanges within a
trusting, intentional community. Guided exploration
groups can be very facilitative.

The Contemplative Approach to Spiritual Direction

I am especially expectant that the contemplative
approach to spiritual direction can prove to be an
effective way to advance seminarians' readiness.
Spiritual direction can most simply be seen as
assistance offered a person who is developing a
relationship with God. A very helpful fuller
definition is:

> help given by one Christian to another which
> enables that person to pay attention to God's
> personal communication to him or her, to respond
> to this personally communicating God, to grow in
> intimacy with this God, and to live out the
> consequences of the relationship.[7]

The contemplative approach to such guidance
emphasizes the act of contemplation, which is looking
at or listening to something, in this case God. This
may be understood more clearly in terms of
functioning:

> What are the most fundamental tasks of the
> director?

> Let us propose that there are two, and that they
> issue from this insight: the contemplative core
> of prayer and of all Christian life is conscious
> relationship with God. The tasks are:

First, helping the directee pay attention to God
as he reveals himself;

Second, helping the directee recognize his
reactions and decide on. . .responses to this
God.[8]

The contemplative theme is consistent with the
injunction repeatedly heard in the gospels and
epistles to keep awake and watch. To contemplate God
with concentrated attention--or simply to do
something with a consciousness of doing it with
God--is very likely to bring forgetfulness of self
and surroundings and to enhance absorption in the
other. Perceptions of God and self and the world
commonly become more clear.
    Specific recommendations for entering such a
practice have been provided by spiritual masters over
the ages. One who gave outstanding directions for
this kind of contemplative prayer and contemplative
spiritual direction was Ignatius of Loyola, in his
Spiritual Exercises. Ignatius emphasized the importance of approaching with an attitude of reverence,
openness and wonder; deciding what is desired and
asking the Lord for it; sharing thoughts and feelings
in intimate, trusting prayer. He next urged waiting
to notice what impressions come in the minutes and
days following, attempting to discern what comes from
the divine, being willing to be surprised by unex-
pected insights, feelings and states, and being ready
to participate in further prayer dialogue.
    The continuous element in such practice is atten-
tion to the reality and nature of God and the
person's relationship with God, allowing it to lead
wherever it will in inner and outer living characterized increasingly by freedom for both the person and
God. God may for any individual at any given time
seem to have most reality as Creator, Parent,
Redeemer, Jesus the friend, infusing Spirit, Judge,
Lover, Liberator, Inspirer, absent, present,
etcetera.
    There are other meanings of the word contempla-
tion. There is the specialized application used by
some to describe a spontaneous mystical state rather
than a practice, for example. According to this

concept, after practicing a purifying, disciplined and one-pointed dwelling on God in the heart, a person may effortlessly shift into an experience of unthinking and unimagining balance, stillness, well being, love, union with the I Am in the center of the person's being. Contemplation is what this experience is sometimes called.

An early description of such consciousness was given in the twelfth century by Hugo of St. Victor, sometimes called the theologian of mysticism. He delineated three stages of prayer as: cogitatio, perceiving God through rational reflection; meditatio, the affective way of turning inward to the heart and meditating on the imago dei that is stamped on the soul; and contemplatio, the intuitive awareness of the divine presence. Walter Hilton referred in the next century to three stages, describing the third as "love on fire with contemplation," while Jan Ruysbroeck described the third as losing oneself in "the darkness of contemplation."[9]

Such a notion of contemplation is regarded in this study as a reality which is experienced by some practiced pilgrims and is related to the goal of spiritual direction. My references to contemplation, however, mean in the broad Ignatian sense (and prevalent Middle Ages sense) simply looking at God--moving beyond concern about subjective issues to giving attention to God, God's action, and relationship with God. This type of regard can embrace reading, meditation, prayer and reverent living. It includes a watchful attitude, a yearning heart, generous self-disclosure and self-surrender, and relational prayer wrestling, as well as absorption in the Beloved.

The methods and the transcendental experiences are contemplative within the all-pervading personal communication with God who is contemplated. The approach to spiritual guidance is called contemplative in that the guide helps facilitate this process, while s/he is also engaged personally in attention to the divine. The expected outcome is a contemplative life in action that is increasingly realistic, obedient and free.

A director will commonly need to help a person to look beyond self toward something outside until the person learns to become absorbed enough to transcend

ordinary consciousness. Nature and Scripture are
notably favorable focuses for contemplation. Others
to which people sometimes turn include public worship, literature, art, music, dreams, journal writing
and drawing, exercise, body sensations, luminous
other people, and noticing what God has done in their
personal lives. A retreat setting or at least
solitude is very conducive.

At the same time, this approach to prayerful
relationship is not passive. It is dialogic and
affective (involving affection and feelings). It
entails the person's desiring to become transparent
to God, generously presenting the whole self, honestly giving full expression to all feelings and
thoughts that are consciously present, as with a
treasured friend. It commonly brings changes in
other parts of living as well--in perceptions,
attitudes, relationships and active involvements, all
experienced from the standpoint of traveling with
God.

Spiritual direction is a form of pastoral care,
but is different from pastoral counseling, even
though the two practices have some features in
common. Pastoral counseling has developed mostly
along the lines of a medical model with a clinical
concern about crisis management. It is generally
applied to help people resolve certain problems and
make more satisfactory adjustments to society.
Spiritual guidance, in contrast, is more growth-
oriented and is not restricted to people with
emotional distress or other specific problems as it
helps people come into more intimate, conscious
prayer association with God. Whereas pastoral
counseling frequently explores the unconscious and
usually aims at a therapeutic end of self-understanding and -determination, often emphasizing attention
to the client's relationship with the counselor, the
spiritual director regularly points beyond self to
exploration of the mysteries of the divine, to discerning and moving with the Spirit.[10]

The term "director" is widely misleading and
off-putting, unfortunately. It carries connotations
of one person's exercising authority to tell another
person what to do, with little emphasis on listening
and much on teaching, preaching and moral guidance.

In fact, we must regretfully admit that such has far too often been the case, and continues to be a temptation for most people in ministries. The heartening reality is that the widespread consensus in training centers currently is to stress fostering a person´s own discovery of the divine grace and will. The shift is typified by a priest who recently described talking with a sister who was agonizing over whether she should stay in her religious order or leave. The priest observed,

> If I were where I was ten years ago, I´d say to her, "Hey, why don´t you go ahead and leave your community?" That was what it was like when I was a spiritual director with emphasis on "director." This time, instead, I focused on how she and the Lord could make the decision together, rather than on my agenda.

When the process is working at its best, both the director and the directee know that their interactions are being directed by the Spirit of the Christ. There are other terms in use for this position—including spiritual guide or friend, soul friend or companion—which also have their usefulness and their limitations.

Spiritual Formation of Seminarians

Spiritual formation "can be understood as the process of allowing the liberation of the real, unique ´Christ form´ within us."[11] When it is pursued by seminary students, the process naturally exhibits some characteristic patterns different from those of the general population. Alan Jones offers these observations.

> . . .seminary communities tend to attract people who sometimes display warring characteristics: a low self-esteem and a high idealism.
>
> Members of such a community react in a variety of ways to this state of affairs. Rage, hurt and disappointment with the failed ideal often take on the form of an "unholier than thou" attitude
> . . . .

Another reaction, which also springs from
disappointment and contempt, is a "holier than
thou" attitude.

Clair McPherson ('82) compared the seminary to a
home for displaced children: "uprooted, angry,
frustrated, lonely, un-trusting, frightened people
brought into a muddle." . . .The flowering of the
genuinely spiritual life is concerned with the
development of our fully human identity in Christ.
. . .One thing is certain. You will begin to
appear--a you "you hardly knew existed." . . .

A great deal of harm is done when the so-called
academic life is divorced from the so-called
spiritual life. Theology and prayer occupy one
domain, not two.

There is no more powerful agent for moral action
than the person who knows who he or she is.[12]

There are some echoes of Jones' assessment in
James W. Fowler's descriptions of moving through six
stages of faith. Fowler identifies typical movement
into and through his Stage 4 as taking place between
late adolescence and the forties, which covers the
age span of most seminary populations. He notes
that:

Where genuine movement toward stage 4 is underway
the person must face certain unavoidable ten-
sions: individuality versus being defined by a
group or group membership. . .self-fulfillment or
self-actualization as a primary concern versus
service to and being for others; the question of
being committed to the relative versus struggle
with the possibility of an absolute. . . .

Stage 4's ascendant strength has to do with its
capacity for critical reflection on identity
(self) and outlook (ideology). Its dangers inhere
in its strengths: an excessive confidence in the
conscious mind and in critical thought and a kind
of second narcissism in which the now clearly

bounded, reflective self overassimilates "reality"
and the perspectives of others into its own world
view.

. . .Disillusionment with one's compromises and
recognition that life is more complex than Stage
4's logic of clear distinctions and abstract
concepts can comprehend, press one toward a more
dialectical and multileveled approach to life
truth.[13]

Sharon Parks, who also is a professor in the field
of spiritual development, gives direct application of
growth stages to seminary experiences:

A change in our theology compels a change in our
experience of prayer. . . . When that which has
been "God" for us is transformed. . .we are moved
from the affective experience of dependence on
assumed authority through counter-dependence, to
an initially fragile inner-dependence (when
authority is still located without but is confirmed within) to a confident inner-dependence
(when the locus of authority is located within yet
confirmed without). There is then the potential
for an inter-dependence, the nature of which I
believe Buber has tried to capture for us in his
notion of the I-Thou relationship. . . .

It should be evident that persons come to theological education at differing moments in this
faith journey. But it is my perception that our
students typically seek theological education at
the moment of emerging inner-dependence and prob-
ing commitment--the moment in faith development I
term "young adult."

. . .If the professions which require theological
education are to be compelling vocations in the
modern world, dialogue with lived experience must
stand at the core of our curricular designs.[14]

These assessments by Jones, Fowler and Parks of
the formation process as it specifically applies to
seminary students add urgency to the need for
providing competent help with the process. They

28

suggest that the students will grow into more mature, whole persons, with a more sturdy faith base on which to launch into ministries if they are provided with spiritual direction that is effective.

Questions Raised

It must be recognized, of course, that some seminarians are mature enough, and inwardly free enough, and spiritually stirring enough to be able to benefit maximally from such guidance, while some others are not. In the A.T.S.-Shalem research done with faculty and staff members, it was found: "A number of participants note the serious problem of attending spiritual development amidst the great academic pressures put on students by most curricula, which tend to choke out or remove to the periphery serious concern for an integral faith life." "A related issue focuses on student capacity. Can you teach depth spirituality to the average young age group we engage? How can we open spirituality to those whose experience in ministry is still too limited to drive them to see the need for it?"[15]
Distinctive questions are raised by representatives of each of the three major traditions included in the research:

Roman Catholic. . . .Some faculty complain of student passive-dependency that, among other things, hinders continuing development after leaving seminary, and an unhealthy introversion rather than other-directedness among some students. . . . The personal readiness and maturity of students sometimes seems inadequate to sustain deep spiritual awareness, regardless of structured opportunities and requirements. . . .

Evangelical. These schools often gather a broad denominational mix of students, which one faculty person describes as particularly valuable to the spiritual formation process.

On the whole these schools seem to have faculties that individually are more committed to involvement in a spiritual formation process with students than is normally true with the other two groupings. . . .

Liberal. The greatest ambivalence and tension concerning spiritual formation is apparent in those Protestant schools that would claim this label. . . .The historic religious practices are ignored or derided in favor of psychological practices rationalized into a Christian context. . . .Spirituality tacitly is seen by many members of these faculties as Pietism taken pejoratively: uncritical, privatistic, sentimental, and detrimental to authentic social and theological analysis and action.[16]

The questions raised in each of these traditions are worthy of serious consideration. The crossfertilization afforded by conversations taking place among representatives of all three, plus the Eastern Orthodox tradition, is particularly welcome and mutually enhancing. It must be clear to us that seminary student bodies in recent years have become increasingly higher in average age, and increasingly balanced by genders and cultural backgrounds. Such factors create an ever-expanding favorable climate for students to seek out, welcome and profit from spiritual guidance.

Urban Holmes, referring to the fifteenth century theologian Jean Gerson, infers that such guidance potentially enhances not only readiness for ministry, but even theological studying in preparation for readiness:

The cognitive domain is a legitimate approach in preparation of the person to be ravished by God, but the affective domain is the sine qua non of the experience of God, which aids a person to think in truer fashion.

Gerson's test for the authenticity of a claim for experience of God is this: if we experience the love of God and there is no transformation of our imagination, mind or will--if we do not surrender ourselves to the other, come to understand that the mind has no immediate knowledge of God or anything else, and live for (transcendent) values --then our claim is in vain. In other words, there is a bond between the excellence of

spirit and of mind. They authenticate one another. .
. . Gerson sums all this up in defining mystical
theology as "wisdom; it is a savory notion possessed
concerning God, when the highest point of reason is
joined and united to him by affective power."[17]

Movements in Some Schools

It is on the basis of such rising insights and shifts
of consciousness that a number of Protestant schools
have been making bold or tentative moves toward the
field of spiritual direction for students and
faculty. Andover Newton has invited a few area
pastors to be available on campus weekly for students
who want to seek their counsel, and one of the
faculty carries a load of seven directees. About
sixty students have attended each time in response to
an invitation from President and Mrs. Peck to come to
their home for a series in which he and a few other
faculty are describing their faith journeys. Princeton has appointed a Pastor to the Seminary, San
Francisco and Chicago a Chaplain. Gordon-Conwell is
currently studying such a post. A Pastor in Resi-
dence who is invited each year by both Chicago and
Pittsburgh may sometimes provide some spiritual
guidance. Pacific School conducted a careful exploration into what spirituality means for faculty,
alumni, students, prospective students and dropouts.
It, like Lancaster, for a time provided a Roman
Catholic religious to aid its students' formation.
The Dean of Students now maintains a list of Roman
Catholic and Protestant qualified guides to whom to
refer individual students making inquiries. She has
facilitated small spiritual formation groups on
request, and has sponsored some introductory evenings
on spiritual guidance, led by a group of spiritual
directors.

Episcopal Divinity and General offer both staff
members and priests from a monastery as spiritual
guides. Harvard makes a Protestant certified
spiritual director available to its students.
Lancaster had a Jesuit priest direct a foundation-
financed Religious Formation Project, which involved
students in mandatory weekly collegia for mutual
learning and support, in retreats and a Seminar in
the Development of Spiritual Theology.

The Project also unsuccessfully attempted to recruit and train ten pastor/preceptors and faculty persons to be spiritual directors.

Fuller instituted a Tri-Phased Formation Program, and encourages M.Div. students to participate for three consecutive years in its courses, small groups, one-to-one monthly meetings with pastors, professors or administrators who act as spiritual directors, and its third year program of prayer partners. San Francisco has established a Center for Christian Spiritual Disciplines, with a focus on Christ-centered spirituality, for people inside and outside the Seminary, to evaluate Christian devotional traditions, discover fresh ways of understanding contemporary spiritual searching, and create Protestant approaches to spiritual counseling with emphasis on preparation of "faithful friends."

The Perkins School of Theology, at Southern Methodist University, inaugurated in the fall of 1983 an experimental program of spiritual formation, using an adaptation of the traditional Methodist class meeting that was developed by John Wesley. The entering class was divided into fourteen weekly groups of seven for pass/fail credit, each one led by a staff or faculty member who did not necessarily have any training for such a function. The school has, together with these groups for juniors, provided four daily opportunities for worship, beginning with 7:30 a.m. Eucharist and ending with 10 p.m. Compline, mostly student-led and lasting ten to thirty minutes.

There most likely are numerous other movements on seminary campuses not mentioned here. My central hypothesis that seminarians generally will be more ready to enter into effective ministries if they have had specific assistance with their personal spiritual formation is clearly far from original with, or peculiar to, me. The Spirit that reconciles intellect and heart into one whole is advancing with power, bringing healing for the dehumanizing alienation of our parts that we have permitted and abetted, especially since the advent of the counterfeit Enlightenment of the eighteenth century.

Thomas Merton expressed the potential arrestingly:

Dogmatic and mystical theology, or theology and "spirituality" are not to be set apart in mutually exclusive categories, as if mysticism were for saintly women and theological study were for practical but, alas, unsaintly men. This fallacious division perhaps explains much that is actually lacking both in theology and spirituality. But the two belong together, just as body and soul belong together. Unless they are united, there is no fervor, no life and no spiritual value in theology, no substance, no meaning and no sure orientation in the contemplative life.[18]

When so many seminaries are providing so richly for the academic and practical preparation of their students, it is spirituality that makes its return now to complete the trinity required for them to be adequately ready when the church sends them forth to provide life-giving ministry. What could be more important, more central to the needs of our day?

The Research Project Design

Since I have long carried an eager concern about the spiritual needs of seminarians, it was natural that I formulated a question for a research project that might help to advance seminaries in this field. I next received consent from three teachers to serve as Director and Readers on my Project Committee and submitted to them a Proposal for the Project.

I then needed to secure permission from one or more seminaries to offer my ministry on their campuses, and to make contact with students who would like to meet with me in spiritual direction. After corresponding with five schools in the Boston area, I had personal interviews with Professor Sharon Parks at Harvard Divinity School and with then Dean George Peck at Andover Newton Theological School. I told them that I believed a study with the focus of my project had never been done, that the need for it was pressing, and that it hopefully would benefit both their institutions and some of their students. Both of them graciously granted the permission.

Dr. Parks personally referred to me the three students I saw at Harvard. Although I posted a bulletin board notice on the campus at Andover Newton, the first three of my students there came to me through off-campus recommendations, one of them in turn guided three others to me, and a professor referred one. The majority of these ten either did not know each other or were not aware that the others were meeting with me. Aside from four of the students, with whom I met only three to ten times, I met with the directees on a weekly basis when school was in session, from the fall of 1982 through mid-May of 1983. Harvard provided an honorarium on a per-session basis, made possible by an anonymous gift intended to be used for a pilot project of providing spiritual guidance to students. The Andover Newton students gave me offerings according to their ability. All of the ten asked for help in: 1) developing a fuller personal relationship with God, and 2) becoming spiritually adequate to take up their intended ministries.

I proceeded to work with the students following these assumptions, as set forth in my Proposal:

• It is part of God's purpose to be in intimate relationship with each of God's children.

• There are spiritual practices that help a person to notice and respond to God's overtures for relationship. These include contemplative prayer which focuses on Scripture, worship, sacraments, nature, dreams, music, physical movement, fasting, retreat, interpersonal relationships, and also includes reflection on everyday living and responding to God's initiatives and imperatives in personal and social realms.

• A trained spiritual director is capable of helping to facilitate this process in a willing person.

- God can work in the process of spiritual direction so that a directee develops progressively in an understanding of call, gifts and limitations, and in enabling for ministry.

- A continuing experience of direct communication with God is of major importance for a person who is to engage in Christian ministry.

My primary criteria for gauging each directee's readiness for ministry were: 1) his/her self-perception, and 2) my perception, of growth in the following areas:

- conviction of call by God to ministry

- sense of his/her specific form of ministry

- concern for, and ability to relate openly with, other people especially in reference to their Christian faith and living

- strength of Christian faith for proclaiming the gospel to others

- awareness of God's active presence in the world

- personal experiencing of ongoing relationship with God that affects his/her personal outlook and conduct

- ability to recognize how the Bible (especially the life and ministry of Jesus) addresses his/her own life and the lives of other persons and groups

- pursuing a balanced and disciplined "rule of life" that includes prayer and worship and that provides personal nourishment for ministering to others

- recognition of gifts s/he possesses that are required for her/his ministry

These same criteria can apply for the exercise of a lay disciple's ministry.
I incorporated these criteria into intake and termination questionnaires that I used with the

students. (Please see the Appendix.) The use of the
questionnaires proved valuable and revealing, especially as a means of helping to objectify and summarize information beyond the perceptions of the
directees and of myself through ongoing sessions.
When I administered the intake version of the questionnaire, I explained that this was related to a
D.Min. project having to do with spiritual direction
for seminary students, but gave no idea of the
specific subject. Even after receiving back the
termination versions, I did not explain unless asked.
I recorded careful notes following all direction
sessions.
After tabulating and reflecting on the questionnaires
in light of my central question and hypothesis,
assumptions and criteria, I arrived at the results,
conclusions and recommendations that are set forth in
Chapter IV.

CHAPTER III:

Four Case Studies

Introduction

The most telling way I can demonstrate the value of
spiritual direction for Protestants is to describe
the process that four specific students and I
experienced together. Of the ten seminarians with
whom I met in spiritual direction, the four described
here are students with whom I met an adequate number
of times (between fourteen and twenty-five), and who
presented issues having to do with readiness for
ministry, earnestly engaged in the process, evidenced
clear progress and who represent a variety of movements. The studies are of three women and one man.
Their age range spans almost twenty years. None had
had an ongoing relationship with a spiritual director
before.

I feel a large respect and affection for each of
these persons. I am very conscious of the sacredness
of being invited into each one's intimate process of
actualizing the Christ Self, and of discerning and
pursuing the highest calling and gifts possible to
make this life count to the fullest for humanizing/
divinizing the journeys of others on this pained
planet.

It is important to present each person's pilgrimage as accurately and faithfully and lovingly as this
special person deserves. At the same time, it is
important to guard confidentiality. My method,
accordingly, is to fictionalize descriptions of
secondary characteristics while precisely reporting
the individual's struggles with God and with living,
even incorporating verbatim bits of our conversations.

Each case study includes a brief description of
the student's appearance and personality, reasons for
entering spiritual direction, relationship with God,
spiritual practices and sense of vocation. Then we

follow this individual through months of living in
dialogue with God, often with a mixture of yearning
and reluctance. The conclusion of each study is the
student's verbal and written commentary about how
this contemplative approach to spiritual direction
affected personal readiness for ministry, in terms of
the several individual factors which the student
identified at our beginning in the fall. My posi-
tioning of each case in the series was governed by a
progression in contrasting issues and developments.
It happens, coincidentally, that there is also a
progression from the person with whom I met the least
number of times to the person with the highest number
of times.

Elizabeth

A pretty, sturdily built, light-haired woman of 34,
Elizabeth gave me the immediate impression of being
bright, lively, inquisitive and interested in the
people around her. She was engaged enthusiastically
in her first year of seminary studies. At the same
time, she was traveling each weekend to a field
education position in the well-known Pilgrim Church
in one of Boston's south shore communities. Her
assignments there were primarily to do pastoral
visitation, to work with the Peace Priority Committee
and to participate in leading worship.
    Elizabeth began the spiritual direction process
with some ambivalence. She was unsure initially
about what spiritual direction was. She felt some
anxiety about having a male director, since she was
working on resolving conflicts with her father that
had gotten in the way of her relating with other
men. However, a fellow student and her field
education supervisor, recognizing that her Christian
faith and her call to ministry were both very
important to her and the subjects of earnest questioning, had recommended me to her. She was struggling to overcome a former false humility and accept
her own value that others affirmed, and to cease
demanding perfection of others and of herself. The
goals that she stated for our meetings together were
to love God more in a closer relationship, and to
actualize more of her true being.

Her initial description of her faith stance was
that she had known herself to be a born-again
Christian, ever since a vivid conversion experience
twelve years before, even though she felt uncomfor-
table using such language. She was having difficulty
articulating her relationship with God in her
theology course. She wrote on her intake questionnaire that "God is wholeness. Divine Parent, Father,
Mother. God is triune and One, God is loving,
mysterious, awesome." By our third session, she
revealed that she had intellectualized God and needed
to liberate God from her own symbolization.

Her prayers were mainly intercessions for other
people. She was reluctant to talk with God about
their relationship and her gifts and direction. She
said:

I feel afraid to get intimate with God, lest God
put a demand on me to sacrifice too much, even to
become a martyr, or to go on a mission to India.
Maybe I'll lose my personal identity if I become
fully used as a vessel of Christ. At the same
time, I'd like it if God would show me more
clearly what all of my potential strengths are,
and what I'm to do with them, and why God brought
me to seminary. I think God sees me as beautiful,
acceptable, valuable, and created for a particular
service, but I need more specifics. How can I
minister to others unless I have confidence and
peace within myself? Sometimes, in my conflicts,
I feel like the children of Israel in the exodus,
wanting the meat of Egypt instead of the manna of
the wilderness.

After two months, Elizabeth was daring occasionally to be more openly personal in speaking to God
about her feelings, and to listen more. She received
the impression that God was feeling her suffering,
and was longing to be in a more intimate relationship
with her. When she preached a sermon at Pilgrim
Church, after prayerful preparation, she discovered
that she had been preaching to herself: "Allow God
to love you. God forgives you, and so you can
forgive. God affirms your womanhood, and so you can,
too, regardless of the contrary images imposed on you
by your mother and the radical feminists on campus."

She repeatedly commented on how important it was
to her to be meeting regularly with me, in spite of
her time pressure from courses and seemingly slow
progress with dropping her ego-centered preoccupation
with herself. Our weekly sessions helped to keep her
conscious of God and the spiritual level in her life,
gave her a feeling of support from a Christian friend
and evoked insights that she wouldn't have been
honest enough to accept on her own. She perceived
that our work had progressed to a deeper level by the
third month. It was only through it, for example,
that she had recognized how relationships with other
people are unavoidably intertwined with her relationship with God, expanding her opportunities to love
God and others and herself.

Even in the face of agonies about course work,
placement interviews and sermon preparation, she
continued to feel resistant to confiding in God.
When I asked her whether she had expressed each
anxiety to God or directly asked whether God wanted
her to be ordained, she admitted that she had not.
Here is a piece of our exchange:

Forster: You wonder, but you haven't asked. How
would you feel about asking if God would like you
to be in ordained ministry?
Elizabeth: It makes sense, sure. In a way,
though, it seems OK to live with some anxiety
instead.
Forster: Maybe you'd rather live with that uncertainty than to ask God?
Elizabeth: In a way, yeah. I'm not sure if I
want to ask. It seems kinda scary. God might ask
something of me that I'm not ready to give.

In our next session she took another step:

Elizabeth: I've chosen as my theme for Lent the
overcoming of anxiety with truth. I realize that
I've been intentionally choosing anxiety-death-
intellect rather than truth-life-heart. I see,
too, what advantages there supposedly were in
holding on to my anxiety, along with trying-
working-proving-controlling.

God led her, she believed, to encounters with just
the right combination of people, including a professor and her field education supervisor, who became
treasured role models. And it was turning out, by
grace, that she actually was doing very well with the
threatening challenges. These experiences were rein-
forcing her self-acceptance and confidence, until she
thought of herself as in a new period of resurrected
life.

Elizabeth stated, "I want ordination so much that
I can hardly stand it." Then she added that she felt
a pressing call to be active helping with social
justice issues. She resolved that she would stay
with her Lenten wilderness of confusion and ask God
to reveal needed insights.

By the time of our termination in mid-May, Elizabeth described herself convincingly as having realized solid progress toward her goals, and in other
areas as well. She identified her primary goal
toward the end of our meetings as "abiding more in
Christ, with action issuing more from prayer and
intentional silence." She named her spiritual
practices the same way at the end as at the beginning, with three exceptions. Both times, she
listed: "prayer, silence, reading Scripture and
other inspirational writings, writing in a journal."
At the end she added: "watching dreams, listening to
others, seeing God in the ordinary."

The following--b., d., f., h. and i.--are the
issues in her readiness for ministry that she singled
out from the intake questionnaire as areas in which
she needed more clarity. Her own written and oral
termination observation immediately follows each
issue named below, indicating ways in which the
spiritual direction process made a difference in her
readiness.

b. A sense of your specific form of ministry

I don't want to be specific right now--I need to
keep myself open to receive that sense of speci-
ficity in time, although I'm feeling increasing
confidence. Spiritual direction has helped me to
feel OK that the clouds didn't part and God

said, "I want you." I feel better and know more strongly that God speaks to me through others—— many others have affirmed my call horizontally——the individual other and the Church others.

d. Strength of your Christian faith for proclaiming the gospel to others

This whole experience has been a Yes experience ——to freedom for myself by which and through which I can invite others to the Good News. Spiritual Direction has helped me to be more comfortable with my faith language. Forster has been a midwife to my articulation which makes me more comfortable with others.

f. Personal experience of an ongoing relationship with God that affects personal outlook and conduct

I am a woman of great Christian faith. I "know" God is with me in a deeper way. My image of God is "Bigger" than it was. There´s more me in God—— as I see more Imago Dei in me. God is omnipresent ——Peace——Imaginative Cosmic Laughter—— Mother Nurturer——Sufferer——Self-emptying empowerer. I have no specific "old man or Sugar Daddy" pictures. Through praying to Christ I <u>know</u> the reality of God.

h. Pursuing a disciplined prayer and worship life that provides personal nourishment for ministry with others

I´m developing the space that feeds myself and others. I´m much more experienced in using spiritual tools now. It´s amazing how a morning Psalm can address the very issue I´m struggling with. I´m only learning to see Jesus and His story directly from Bible context to mine——I <u>know</u> there is synthesis but only beginning to name <u>it.</u>

i. Recognition of gifts you possess that are required for your ministry

An ongoing process--I do listen better having had
Forster to dialogue with. Out of the turmoil and
beauty of my searching, I am feeling more able to
affirm the goodness of sexuality and celebrate my
femaleness, as part of the way my inner self can
be used most positively in ministry. I am much
stronger in self-esteem, less troubled with guilt.

Kathy

It is impressive to discover how much Kathy has
already experienced and thought about at the age of
23. Early in our series of meetings, as I watched
the animation in her slender face surrounded by
auburn hair, I found myself easily engaged by her
spiritual yearning, her facile mind, her creative
turn of phrase. It was quickly evident, too, that
she felt no compulsion to conform her thinking to
that of the seminary faculty or the authorities in
her United Methodist Church district, even though she
accepted their stimulating ideas or reasonable
policies.

While active in the feminist movement at Smith
College, Kathy had found that pursuit incompatible
with faith, worship and personal prayer, and so had
given up her spiritual life for many months. Since
then she had stayed with a subsequent decision to be
a low-key feminist and also a searcher for God. She
had briefly been a member of a charismatic prayer
group and found that it was not right for her. She
had taken a year after college to try working in big
business and to carry on an active social life in
Philadelphia, and was now devoting her energies to
being her own woman, and a woman in Christ.

She stated three goals for spiritual direction at
the outset, based on what she called an acute need--
"even terror would not be too strong a term to use":

1) Maintain conscious soul communication with
God, in contrast with academic courses that make
no place for this dimension, and with a fairly
prevailing campus suspicion of language like
"knowing the Lord through prayer";

2) relate these two worlds, employing both my
soul and my intellect (e.g. find words to articulate the spiritual dimension in the King David
stories);
3) develop a regular discipline of prayer and
find the authority of my own prayer and imagery of
God.

Kathy described God, in one approach, as the
center of the circle of life in the universe. The
parts of the universe are spatially separate from
God, yet "the center defines the shape of the circle,
in fact gives existence to ´all things visible and
invisible.`" On a more visceral level, she spoke of
personally feeling God´s presence, experiencing
closeness and exchange and guidance. "Jesus Christ
is the sign of God´s presence, his life is the
narration of what happens to servants of God, and his
love is what makes me, in spite of possible conse-
quences, seek God. In other words, if Jesus could
serve, suffer and love, God must be worth the
effort."
Kathy´s prayers, when we began, were sporadic,
"usually in times of desperation." The problem that
she perceived in her relationship with God was, "I
continually try to grasp and simplify God, to control
God, and to find out how to earn from God what I most
desire." Her most memorable spiritual experience had
taken place in college when she felt she was falling
in love with another woman, an experience she said
was shattering and "felt at the same time as a true
gift and challenge from God. My rejection of that
love was transformed, at a moment when I was almost
literally mad with terror, by the reassurance of the
presence of God in this and all of life´s surprises." She soon became convinced that her
orientation was heterosexual.
We gave extensive attention in our spiritual
direction process to her prayers and prayer images,
her anger with impersonal professors, her relationship with parents and friends, her own identity, and
her progress toward ordination in fulfillment of a
call. Each area brought satisfactions and conflicts. "´Enduring` is the word that characterizes
the period I´m in right now," she stated in our
second session. She was scarcely two months into the
first year of her seminary career.

44

Kathy asked for a suggestion about what she might do in her devotional periods. When she mentioned that she had recently felt drawn to the early verses of Isaiah 43, we agreed that she would do well to respond to that attraction by asking God to show her whatever she needed to see as she meditated on those words. That evening she learned in prayer that God in truth calls her by name.

Then came an image in her prayer. The Archangel Michael was standing radiantly triumphant over a dragon that he had slain and hewed into pieces. He next was facing God as a shining boy with a look of innocence, like a puppy with a mouse, looking to God for reward. God looked on Michael with forgiving acceptance. God reached out primarily to the other, who was now a half-drowned woman, with restoring love. Kathy saw herself in this image coming before God as two beings. It seemed to her as though God were revealing how destructively she had overvalued the masculinity in her nature, at the expense of a rejected, broken womanhood.

In the following week, she attempted to continue praying with the Isaiah passage, particularly the words, "I have redeemed you," but she reported that her prayers had been flat. What did she want from God now, I asked. She replied, "Not neat answers to my questions. But I would like God to come and sit by me on the floor and help me as I struggle to see how all these recently emerged pieces fit together." Had she asked this? No. Did she want to try? "Maybe. Except that I'm afraid I might receive a different response than I want?" Did she suppose that awareness of this risk might have kept her prayers flat in the past week? "Oh, yes! I'll bet I could have been holding myself back from full open- ness." A similar dynamic of her resistance surfaced soon after this one which helped her to see that resentment against an alienated boyfriend was related to a sense of separation from God.

This conversation took place during session five. By session nine, Kathy was exclaiming about how rapidly her relationship with God and her viewpoints had been changing. After having passed through a period of rage, mostly about the teaching methods of some faculty members, she found a tempering to what she called "disciplined rage," and then more

compromise, resolution and acceptance, so that she
could with integrity remain in seminary. She had
made a clear choice to move forward and be "real,"
that is, be a responsible adult. She was now writing
papers as a real person with her own personal viewpoints. She had prayerfully dealt with fear of
hostility from her radical feminist acquaintances and
dared to help lead a rather traditional liturgy. She
had decided to level with her grandmother about an
annoyance. She experienced less fear and self-rejection when visiting her parents and was even able to
function some as an adult facilitator for her parents' marriage. She noticed that she was no longer
transferring bitter estrangement from her former
boyfriend over to God, was even wishing her ex-friend
well and was trusting God's providence for both of
them, and continued to be sure that God was taking a
loving interest in her affairs.

The subject of the church and her potential part
as an ordained minister within it was one that
frequently occupied her mind, bringing attendant
feelings ranging from confident peace through
outraged fury. She entered seminary as a result of
perceiving, in prayer on a college retreat, that she
was called to the ordained ministry in the United
Methodist Church. Lately she had been fluctuating as
to the specific form of ministry. During periods
when her schooling seemed most sterile, she was
tempted to give up the whole enterprise. When she
raised such complaints in prayer, the response was
that God was sustaining and affirming her. Her
fairly consistent sense during the second term was
that she was called to a ministry of community
building, laying planks in place across various
chasms that separate people.

After a November series of preliminary interviews
with her district committee considering whether to
accept her officially as a candidate for ordination,
Kathy traveled back in March for the determinative
weekend meeting. She came back feeling shattered and
infuriated. The committee had rejected her. Its
impression was that she had a lot of confusion and
uncertainty in her development, was theologically
unformed and had no clear sense of call. She sput-
tered out to me that she considered the committee
members to have been devoid of respect and

sensitivity toward her, demanding too harshly that she submit to the control of the church. She admitted that she had recognized some arrogance in herself as well. As she had been frequently in prayer during the intervening days, she had poured out her feelings and asked for peace, rest, clarity, forgiveness and healing. God seemed very present and active in a loving way, granting her requests.

Within six weeks of the rejection she was able to give thanks for the benefits of growth that she was noticing. She had moved through anger, depression and grief to humility and a readiness to present herself with changed attitudes and positions. She still could not bear the committee's prevalent representation of a four-decker universe made up of God-bishop-district superintendent-priest. The church still seemed on some days like "a 2,000-year-old farce." Nonetheless, she resolved to reapply after the required waiting period. A time of prayer with her roommate helped her toward accepting and loving her seminary and church, living a part of their lives as creatively as she could find the grace to do. She would devote herself to expressing more of what God is—"God, who gives vast freedom but is always gently drawing us back, like a very flexible elastic band around us. Elastic love is needed."

Kathy affirmed, in our final evaluation, that she had come to realize, as we had progressed in our spiritual direction, that what she had needed was "exactly this kind of examining of my issues of current living within the perspective of my relationship with God. I found that my purpose, progress, and confidence were all valuably clarified through this. In fact, I've anticipated our meetings as the high point in my week."

The issues in her readiness for ministry that she singled out as areas in which she needed more clarity are b., c., g., h. and i. on the intake questionnaire. Each one noted here is immediately followed by her written and oral comment at termination time about differences made by having spiritual direction.

b. A sense of your specific form of ministry

The content of my ministry changes continually, and while I feel for the moment that my path has shape, my situation is such, I believe, that many shapes will come and go between now and the next few months. Despite the events of the last period, my sense of call has been unchanged, largely due to the support and interest of my small community, including spiritual direction.

c. Concern for, and ability to relate openly with, other people, especially in reference to their Christian faith and living

In some ways, this part of my life has tightened. I am less tolerant of others, regardless of their position vis-a-vis Christianity. At the same time, I am learning how to take seriously the command to love both enemies and neighbors as self.

My relationship with God feels quite warm and direct, and occupies a place of central importance, but I find it hard to express, and feel a need to protect my experience of God from others. I sense a hostility in my world that threatens to wither my faith with logic or ridicule.

g. Ability to recognize how the Bible (especially the life and ministry of Jesus) addresses your own life and the lives of other persons and groups

No, this is a trouble spot. This is closely related to anxiety about the efficacy of Jesus, as presented in gospels, and as exegeted by scholars, in addressing present crises. Jesus seems to me to be indisputably central. But who was Jesus? And what business does the Church have in claiming the exhaustive presentation of the Christ as it does? And how could anyone who finds the tradition qua tradition deeply and consistently oppressive actually fight through to a proclaimable Jesus at all?

h. Pursuing a disciplined prayer and worship life
that provides personal nourishment for ministry with
others

   Yes and no. Discipline in observance has become
   much less of a priority for me, replaced by
   discipline of staying on the quest for an observance that is liberating and helpful. "Undisci-
   pline" in formal observance has been a necessary
   condition of the journey. that is not to say a
   total lack of formal observance; that would
   likewise be unhelpful. It is simply to say that I
   have chosen to stop forcing myself to cope on a
   regular and committed basis with a tradition I
   find threatening. Right now, I am regular with
   grace at meals, and rather regular with daily
   prayers (sometimes with members of my close
   community) and with fasting, and churchgoing.

i. Recognition of gifts you possess that are
required for your ministry

   This has gone on, thanks to support and affirmation from friends and communities, as well as from
   growing strength of conviction on my own part.
   Also, as ministry becomes less something "other
   than" what I have done in the past, the professional and personal talents I have shown in other
   settings take on more and more visible influence
   in the specific shape of my ministry.

   To these Kathy added the following summary
comment:

   This has been a tough, tough year for me, and
   spiritual direction was an important "track point"
   for the experience. It was a stable point, and I
   could locate myself by bouncing signals off it.
   That has been invaluable.

   Right now I am feeling the burden of 2,000 years
   of Christian history, both as a believer who
   objects to doctrine qua doctrine, and as a woman
   who feels trashed by the whole body of religious
   scholarship. This disillusionment is profound
   enough to seriously affect the shape of my

vocation, though not such as to erase the sense of vocation altogether. Spiritual direction has helped point out appropriate strengths and raise my level of hope, and been sustaining in that sense. I don't know what it might require for me to find some peace with the tradition that would still honor what I affirm as a call to ministry, but is clearly the hottest item on the smorgasbord.

Jim

Jim gave the impression, in our first meeting, of being solidly thoughtful, reticent, reliable. The combination of his sturdy build, medium height, straight black hair, and the steady gaze in his blue eyes represented to me his readiness to proceed, with caution. He had exercised initiative in seeking out a spiritual director, even though such a move was unconventional in his contemporary church practice.

Part of Jim's purpose was to become increasingly emancipated from what he perceived to have been a heavy rigidity of his childhood parish and family. He had acquired his early Christian education in a midwestern parish of the Missouri Synod branch of Lutheranism, which seemed to take the stance of possessing the only true understanding of the Truth in faithfulness to Jesus Christ.

One way of seeking more freedom in early adulthood had been to apply his keen intellectual ability in the field of natural science, earning a master's degree in microbiology. He was now approaching religion somewhat from the rational scientific view-point, particularly enjoying a course on theology, and another on eastern religions. There was along with that another movement in his nature, which had led him to human service work with disadvantaged people for a couple of years. He was attempting at the same time, with some difficulty, to allow himself to reach out socially and take time for fun with friends. He had, in the last few years, felt in-creasingly drawn to religion, made frequent visits to a Christian residential community, and become a member of a progressive parish of the American Lutheran Church.

A close friend has made repeated comments to him
that he would like it in a seminary. After consider-
able resistance, he came to a sense that this was one
of several signs of God's wanting him in ordained
parish ministry. Now, in his middle thirties, he was
in his second year of preparation, in a non-Lutheran
school.

When I asked why he wanted to be in spiritual
direction, Jim answered, in part, that he had lately
been less self-enclosed and less wary of trusting
others, and more willing to follow his intuition
which told him that God's active presence in life was
real. He put his three goals in writing this way:

I am looking for some guidance in learning to
recognize God's presence and activity in my
life--also, for guidance in my struggle with
believing there is a God. A bit more superfi-
cially, spiritual direction might nudge me into
being more faithful to spiritual disciplines.
More clarity in my vocation would be good, too.

Beginning with our very first meeting, Jim set
himself earnestly about keeping a period for morning
devotions almost daily, in spite of troublesome
doubts and a welter of mental distractions. He
typically found it helpful to meditate on a passage
of Scripture and let it speak to him, sometimes
employing the Ignatian approach of imagining himself
to be present and addressed. It was also typical
that, as soon as it seemed that he might be in touch
with the divine, something in him would remonstrate,
"How absurd! Maybe there's no God there at all."

Over a number of weeks, he spent time with Psalms
139, 103 and 34, Jeremiah and Lamentations 2, Acts,
and Hebrews 12. He frequently prepared for prayer by
chanting a canon, occasionally turned to a mantra
such as the Jesus Prayer, and generally finished by
writing a journal entry. There were evenings when he
and his fiancee, Meg, did chanting and prayers
together. He developed a cautious willingness to try
speaking his honest views and feelings in prayer,
including skepticism, thankfulness, lustful temptations, the need for guidance in leading his youth
group. He liked to lift up praise to God, welcoming
the assistance of the psalmist: "Bless the Lord, O

my soul;/and all that is within me, bless his holy
name!"; or, "For thou didst form my inward parts,/
thou didst knit me together in my mother's womb./ I
praise thee, for thou art fearful and wonderful."[1]

When I asked him, in session two, what God seemed
like to him as he prayed with a psalm, Jim said that
God seemed to be more passive than active, non-
judging, accepting him as he was. He then revealed
how his early religious training had conditioned his
image of God. According to that, God requires him to
be serious, hard-working, "satisfactory" in terms of
others' expectations (his father's word) and not
playful or sexual. Another of the phrases that Jim's
father characteristically used was, "Don't be
silly." Part of him believed that such attitudes and
phrases must not be true to God's view. Possibly God
even likes it when he and his fiancee arouse feelings
of sexual excitement in each other. This was too
much to seem real altogether, even though he was
attempting to break out of old life-denying confine-
ments. When I asked if he would like to ask God
directly about these wonderments, he said he would.
In fact, though, he did not get around to it.

In his distress about whether he ever would be
able to discern a call from God to ministry, it
helped him to hear a professor's sermon on Jeremiah's
call. Like Jeremiah, Jim was raising objections:
not being gregarious, a people's person, uncertain
whether he ever had genuine contact with God or if
God actually existed or cared. However, he did
recognize some relevant abilities that he had to
offer: caring, listening, counseling, studying,
preaching, perceiving the core of an issue, teaching. And there was a continuing sense that he was
"supposed to" be a minister, even though maybe that
was only a part of his karma rather than God's plan.

A further reason for his holding back rose to view
in session eight:

Forster: If you imagine a time when God would
respond to you by giving you some definite impression of being present and wanting to be in a
relationship with you, how do you think you would
react?

Jim: (After silent thought) At first my feeling
would be joy, happiness, confidence, thankfulness,
because I've been hoping for that for so long.
But then very quickly I think I'd find ways to
deny that God had communicated to me that way.
There's something in me, I'm sure, that would be
resistant to God's showing me something like that.
Forster: You'd be resistant. Why do you think
you'd resist?
Jim: It's partly because of the skepticism that
got ingrained in me through my scientific
studies. I think that denying talk about receiving personal messages from God is part of what
I've built in as my identity, that it would be
hard to let go of.
Forster: You wanted that to be part of how you'd
be known.
Jim: Yeah. It's partly in reaction against
hearing dogmatic fundamentalists in my childhood
church talk about personally knowing the Lord, and
my vowing that I'd never be like that. Actually,
I find that I'm embarrassed to talk with anyone in
terms of personal spiritual experience, even with
Meg. She and I can say prayers together, but it's
harder to talk about it. I think that to admit
that I received something from God would feel as
though I were giving in to what I had chosen not
to be in my identity.

Possibly this locating of the problem more specifically had a somewhat freeing effect for Jim. The
next week he reported that he had been taken by surprise when a rather vivid dialogue opened up during a
prayer with the narrative of Jesus' asking His disciples who others and they said He was, and Peter's
reply. As he visualized the scene, before Peter
spoke, Jesus turned to Jim and asked directly who he
said He was. At first he resisted, then gave a
halting, indefinite response.
He was taken by surprise again the following
week. While walking in the woods on a warm December
day, he quickly became absorbed in the trees' shapes
and barks, as though he were in communication with
them in a higher state of consciousness. Feeling
that God was somehow in this experience, he trans-
ferred his attention over to formulating words of

thanksgiving. When he got back to his room, a feeling came spontaneously over him as though he were a minister celebrating the Eucharist.

His next two days' prayers were accompanied again by a brief sense of divine presence, even though the thought arose of how absurd it was for him to suppose it was real. He told me that he was making a decision to pay serious attention to God if more such initmations were given. He added that he felt more secure now in talking with both Meg and me about spiritual experience, so long as he avoided pietistic language. He thought perhaps he was being called to rise above his anti-Missouri Synod reaction and be prepared to experiment with speaking openly about God when occasions seemed to make it appropriate. Another way that he wanted to be more outgoing was by becoming engaged in action for social causes.

Jim reported in March that, on the previous Friday, God had used his studies about salvation to give him by grace a felt realization that in Jesus Christ he is already accepted and restored from estrangement from God. He was able to locate the feeling physically in his chest-diaphragm area. When this came over him, he stopped his studies awhile, just to experience and give thanks for it.

He said in April that, after a couple of months of experimenting with Basil Pennington's style of centering prayer almost daily—even though it had brought seconds at a time of concentrated attention—he felt a lack of the awareness of companionship with God that came through dialogic prayer. Another observation of note was that, even though something in him was quick to say no, he had come briefly to a strong and excited vision of attraction to pastoral ministry of Word and Sacrament. Feedback from people in his field education parish, after he led worship, affirmed this. He realized that he was struggling more to keep hope (as trust) than faith (as belief).

He said in May that he was accepting McQuarry's position that it is more workable to relate with the God of mystery as personal than as impersonal. It was important to avoid getting stuck in the limitations of literalism, keeping analogies and symbols alive in his thought system. He suspected that he was in touch with the "cloud of unknowing." He yearned continually for God's presence.

54

The following--a., b., e., f. and h.--are the
issues in his readiness for ministry that he singled
out from the intake questionnaire as areas in which
he needed more clarity. His written and oral
termination observation immediately follows each
issue named below, indicating ways in which the
spiritual direction process made a difference in his
readiness.

a. Conviction of a call by God to ministry

Spiritual direction has helped me to be attentive
to my searching for a deeper sense of calling, and
to ask God for it. . . .Such a sense of calling to
ordained ministry has been clearly given.

b. A sense of your specific form of ministry

This is a next step. At this point, I feel
settled with a calling into ordained ministry in
general (in the American Lutheran Church), which
will begin in parish ministry. Further specific
forms will unfold when the time is right. . . .
The affirmation of a calling into ordained
Christian ministry has greatly enhanced my readiness to proclaim the Christian faith in word and
sacrament.

e. Awareness of God´s active presence in the world

I am not yet very attentive to God´s active
presence in the world, i.e., beyond my own
personal experience. I have focused more on my
own life and calling during these months of
spiritual direction. It would be good to move
from here to more awareness of God in the lives of
others.

f. Personal experience of an ongoing relationship
with God that affects personal outlook and conduct

I have a deepened yearning for God´s presence. I
have had some times of being more conscious of
that presence and have come to feel comfortable in

addressing God. This still is sporadic, but is much more consistent than when we began. At times I am aware of a greater sense of peace and open- ness to others growing out of this relationship with God.

h. Pursuing a disciplined prayer and worship life that provides personal nourishment for ministry with others

Spiritual direction has been very helpful here. I have developed a fairly regular prayer life and even find myself yearning for it when I miss it. I hope to continue this discipline, although I'm concerned about whether I'll be as regular without seeing you. I appreciated your encouraging me when I was inclined to try new forms, e.g., centering prayer, walking in the woods.

He volunteered these further comments:

In responding to all the areas of #9 (except h) it is hard to identify precisely the impact of spiritual direction. There have been many other factors influencing my spiritual formation. I think that the effect of the spiritual direction experience has been to make me more <u>attentive</u> to those "other factors" (e.g., course-work, conversations with others, field education experiences, etc.) Spiritual direction provided a structure and an aid to recognizing what was taking place for me in my spiritual search—to stay with the struggle and the questioning, to be open to (and ready to receive) responses and insights.

Jackie

Jackie was a senior M.Div. candidate in her late thirties, with a tall, athletic appearance, her long brown hair falling gracefully below her shoulders. She had become disillusioned very early with her father's brutal treatment, her mother's weakness and the male rigidity that she had perceived in the Roman Catholic Church. She learned that she could gain recognition and admiration by excelling in school studies and in sports.

She exercised both her able intellect and her
attuned intuition for eclectic exploring and direct
experiencing. This took her to eastern mysticism,
astrology, native American religion, shamanism,
feminist spirituality, New Age thought, holistic
lifestyles, body work, psychic healing, and an
appreciation of the power of symbols in dreams, art,
music and ritual. The childhood conviction still
persisted in her that she was called to be a priest,
or minister, or shaman.

Now it seemed to be time to reintensify her continuing spiritual search. She knew that her course
work and her many inner experiences were not enough
without a conscious relationship with God. It
impressed her that it could be risky to get closer to
God, though, since it possibly could lead where she
would not choose to go.

Jackie's presenting reasons for entering spiritual
direction were more specific than an undifferentiated
spiritual search. Although convinced that she had
received numerous glimpses of Reality, and was officially in the In Care status as a ministerial
candidate in the Presbyterian Church, she felt
confused by her sense of rejection by the church in
childhood and her studies of other religions. She
was sure that God accepts non-Christians as well as
Christians, and offers them grace. She was honestly
not entirely clear if or how she was a Christian.
She therefore wrote, "I don't want to be confined to
a male god system and spiritual practices from
another time and culture and sex. I don't want an
experience where a system is put onto me from outside, but instead drawn forth from within."

There were three past experiences to which she
made repeated references. She was nine years old
when she had the first two. In the first, feeling
that she was someday to become a priest, she
approached her parish priest and asked to be included
in the class of boys being trained to be altar boys.
The Father laughed and explained that only those
could lead worship who represented the nature of God
as Jesus had done, being male. She then went home
and declared to God that she was through with His
Church. Her second memory from that age was of going
outside in the evening, looking up at the stars,
repeating "Star light, star bright . . .", and then

adding the passionate petition, "Please, God, send someone to love me." The petitions seemed to be in vain.

Her most memorable spiritual experience had come to her seven years before, in a time of severe personal upheaval:

> A dream which "turned my life around". . . after cataclysmic crashing of islands into the sea, I entered the pit in the ocean and was lifted out by a tidal wave in the form of a hand, which destroyed all the rest of the surface of the creation. I awoke knowing that God had been there and that "everything would be all right and as it should have been" now. This greatly changed my perception of my life and gave a kind of hope I had never known.

Two or three years later she decided to try praying again, and soon afterward made her decision for seminary. There were a couple of times when she had been in distress and had called out for help and received it, then had had a hunch that it was the spirit of Jesus who had responded. When I asked if she would like to try to get in touch with Him in quiet and ask who He would like to be to her, she consented. The next week she described awakening early one morning, being unable to return to sleep, then opening and appealing to Jesus. She received a feeling that His hand was on her head. She reported a week later that, since she had opened to Jesus, she had noticed that His presence was steadily with her, behind her left shoulder.

Jackie asked Jesus, through writing a journal dialogue in late October, if she had to be weak in order for Him to accept her (even though she knew herself to be weak as well as assertive). He said no. She asked if she would have to give up her feminist anger (even though she believed that she would need to go beyond some of her angers in time). Jesus replied, "No, love it." It was her impression that Jesus was not exclusively male, but that He included the best of both male and female, as had been true also of several other people whom she perceived to be most spiritually realized. She later told a friend that she thought she was becoming a Christian, which produced copious tears in her.

When, in prayer one evening, she gave herself to
God's guidance and protection, she immediately
reacted with the question, "Is this mindless
dependency, passive femininity?" The reply occurred
to her: "Jackie, you are strong enough to be weak
now. You are strong enough to allow yourself to be
loved. Feeling protected will not make you passive,
but more active."

A later series of events on campus, pressure from
her studies, and a weekend trip left her feeling
alone and hurting. She was angry with God and me and
others. She detected no response in her attempts to
talk with God. Then she had an important dream.
After climbing up a steep precipice to a castle, she
managed to open its large door with ease. She was
welcomed by a tall, slender, dark-haired, regal
woman, who had been awaiting her and treated her as
special, giving her a cup of the castle water.
Reflecting on this dream and others about numinous
women, she thought, "Perhaps they not only represented part of myself, but were God coming to me when
it seemed in my waking life that God was absent."
When she next tried to address God and then Jesus in
writing, without response, she did make connection
when she addressed the regal woman. Through further
meditative reflection, it was shown to her that there
actually had been a dark-haired woman in her outer
life when she was a child and had prayed to God to
send someone to love her. It was her godmother whom
she called Aunt Kate.

She asked if God were in the dark-haired woman.
The reply was that God can come to a person in
innumerable appearances, and that we must beware of
trying to constrict what God can be by our own
preconceptions. She repented of having held onto
skewed images of the divine that had been represented
to her by her childhood priest and others. She
recalled Scripture references to God as woman, a hen
with chicks, a midwife, a comforting mother.

Then, as on numerous other occasions, she commented how glad she was to be seeing me regularly,
since there was so much about God that she would be
missing if she were processing all of her issues
alone. Frequently, after our conversations, she felt
lighter and more ready to deal with her issues in
consciousness that God was in them with her.

Jackie noted, following Easter, that she was not yet resolved about Jesus. She pondered, "Was Jesus only a symbol of transformation, or did He actually alter the balance of the earth, as some claim He did? And is He actually available to us now in personal relationship?"

A lasting, changing image arose to absorb her attention. There was a coffin-like box in a dark basement, chained by its four corners to the corners of the room. This immediately suggested the Jesus held down within her because she was afraid that He might turn out to be like the sweet stereotypes, or she might lose Him if she faced Him. She wondered what else possibly could be in the box. She felt fear and tears about finding out, but wanted to proceed and to give the contents freedom to be whatever they were. She hoped uncertainly that she had an inner wisdom that would prevent her from seeing more than she could handle. Day by day, she imaginatively returned to the image, and developed a ritual of walking around the room, burning sage and cedar for purification, carefully stepping over the chains. When she finally opened the box, she dis-covered the body of a woman, which was almost dead and in the process of reanimation. But she had expected to find Jesus. Could this be a female Christ? Was it her own self? Perhaps they were the same, and both consciously coming alive.

When she prayed about her vocation and watched the evidences of God's moving in her life, most of the time she felt confident that all of the necessary elements would fall into place as needed. Although she was not cognitively sure if she were a Christian, she felt in her soul that she was. She knew that she could not consider ministry in the Unitarian Univer-salist context, as some friends had suggested, because she believed that that denomination had decided not to deal with the issues of Jesus and Scripture, and so had no adequate way of responding "when souls are talking."

By April, she felt much more clear about her direction. She accepted a position in a Th.D. program, in an outstanding midwestern school of theology, in Practical Theology. She would combine her interests in feminist spirituality, the devel-opment of peace churches, and how the Presbyterian

Church might develop in both of these capacities. She hoped that her work could include leading retreats, if she could get to the point of openly guiding people to the Christ within. This thought brought a welling up of tears of longing for such gifted potential. Perhaps the retreatants would help draw the ability out of her.

In May, a month before being graduated, she preached in her home congregation, using explicitly orthodox language, including a statement about Jesus and our salvation. The sermon went very well, with a sense of empowerment. It felt like a clear manifestation of Christian faith, which was evolving into solid conviction. She still felt congruent about it afterward. Even though she still balked at some traditional language, like "Jesus Christ as your Lord and Saviour," she felt joy at wanting to develop more of a relationship with Him. She believed that she could present an acceptable statement if she applied in the future for ordination.

Jackie still saw herself as called to function somehow as a priest, helping people to find the life of God within themselves.

The issues in her readiness for ministry that she selected as areas in which she needed more clarity are a., b., c., d. and h. on the intake questionnaire. Each one noted here is immediately followed by her written and oral comment about differences made by having spiritual direction as we completed our twenty-five sessions.

a. Conviction of a call by God to ministry

My experience in spiritual direction has been in my growing conviction of a call by God in my life. This has been an area of conflict and doubt--wondering about "ego" needs rather than God being the motivation. Direction has helped me make connections that have been disconnected, but there, for quite awhile. Has taken what I felt to be "grandiosity" and shown that to be God's involvement and call, and my own potential for wholeness.

b. A sense of your specific form of ministry

This has been a large part of my work because I
did not feel drawn to parish ministry, and clari-
fication of my desire for further schooling and
experience, toward teaching and denominational
work has been an important part of my direction.

c. Concern for, and ability to relate openly with,
other people, especially in reference to their
Christian faith and living.

I am growing in this as Christian symbols take on
more connection with the deep structures I believe
in. Much of the integrating work my director has
done in listening and feeding back has helped me
gain a feeling of integrity with my use of Christian faith.

d. Strength of your Christian faith for proclaiming
the gospel to others

This is developing as I see my own faith convictions which empower my life as congruent with the
good news of the Christian story. I am just
beginning to do that based on my own convictions
rather than as a mode of thinking I need to
translate into.

h. Pursuing a disciplined prayer and worship life
that provides personal nourishment for ministry with
others

I have mostly developed this on my own. Suggestions of Scripture that seemed relevant to what I
was thinking about were often helpful as well. My
present spiritual practices include: Meditation
in conjunction with writing conversations with
God. Prayer rituals with candles and incense.
Reading inspirational writings. Meditating on the
Acts of the Apostles in Scripture, recording and
exploring my dreams, jogging.

Jackie concluded by volunteering these evaluative
remarks:

Forster:

[Although I sometimes had feelings of frustrations
and lack of trust in you], they were counter-
balanced by the freedom I had to allow the process
I was experiencing to continue, boosted but not
taken over by the talking we did. Your integrating and connecting comments helped me move past or
at least see the ways I was stuck and always led
to further engagement and movement. . . .

I value greatly what part our relationship has had
in my growing sense of relationship with God and
Jesus, and my ever-clarifying sense of priestly
vocation.

CHAPTER IV:

Results, Conclusions, Recommendations

The first purpose of this chapter is to review and
evaluate the gains made in readiness for Christian
ministry through the contemplative approach to
spiritual direction by the four students in this
study. The second is to draw conclusions and offer
recommendations for Protestant seminary education.

Being a secondary participant in the interaction
between God and these beloved pilgrims was frequently
a cause of awe and joy and satisfaction in me. Even
though I have come firmly to expect the intervention
of God´s wise and loving providence in people´s
lives, and even though Jesus´ ask-seek-knock invitation is accompanied by His triple promise, I still am
sometimes astonished when I see divine providence
unfolding before my eyes. It became an increasing
conviction of each participant in this research that,
if a person will make an unqualified, honest appeal
in prayer, and give the time and attentiveness to
receive a response, God will often prove strongly
interested in being a dialogue partner. Although
there was no question on the questionnaires specifically about such a conviction, the experiences
(largely evoked by the spiritual direction process)
that nurtured it in each student were of basic
importance in their advancing readiness.

It will be useful to summarize here some of the
background characteristics of spiritual search and
experience that the students held both in common and
separately during our work together.

Similarities

1. In spiritual journeys:

- Longing to experience more intimate connection with God, and simultaneously holding up barriers to keep God at a certain distance.

- Being able to relate at least one personal experience of God's self-disclosure.

- Hungering for precise blueprints of God's plan for their careers, nevertheless clinging to preconceived vocational images and dislikes of their own.

- Being impatient about not making faster progress in their spiritual searches.

- Sometimes resisting communication with God, lest it yield unwelcome information.

- Engaging in seminary training because they felt drawn toward ministry, although suffering periods of self-doubt and uncertainty about continuing all the way to ordination.

- Experiencing continuing conflicts with parents.

- Remaining consistently conscious of the church's history as oppressor, and making personal efforts to employ sexually inclusive language and to contribute to the ministries of reconciliation in both church and world.

2. In the ways that they made use of spiritual direction, producing growth in:

- Clarity of insights and honesty with themselves.

- Ability to relate trustingly with me and to admit embarrassing goals, dreams, temptations, delusions, resistances, guilts and failures.

- Freedom in approaching, and responding to God; also in allowing God the freedom for self--disclosure and giving personal direction as God chose.

- Facility for recognizing an experience of contact with God, for noticing, identifying and dealing with feelings within themselves as well as thoughts, for expressing feelings and desires to God, then being alert to responses from God.

- Relating their academic building of beliefs about God to their direct prayerful developing of personal rapport with God.

- Awakening to the necessity to move out from a sound intimate spiritual foundation to make contributions to the well being of others—both individual and church others, and those entangled in complex worldly systems.

Differences

These are individualities other than those of age, gender, family and social backgrounds, denominations, seminary classes.

1. Faith identity and goals in spiritual direction:

- Elizabeth, who considered herself a born-again Christian, wanted to love God and actualize her true being.

- Kathy, a conflicted admirer of Jesus, desired to communicate with God, integrate this with academics and develop a discipline and authority of prayer.

- Jim, thinking perhaps he was a Christian, hoped to believe there is a God and recognize God in his life, developing faithful spiritual disciplines and clarity in vocation.

- Jackie, exploring whether it was Jesus Christ who had been involved in her faith experiences, wanted to discover whether Christian symbols were real for her, whether she could use them as a minister and whether she had a call.

2. Images of, and relationships with, God after spiritual direction--all stronger than at the start:

• Elizabeth's image of God was "bigger"--"more me in God and God in me"--and she discerned that revelations in understanding had come from the Paraclete through the Risen One.

• Kathy was attempting less to control God and more to be controlled by God, and Jesus became definitive for her.

• Jim said God was mostly hidden, sometimes visible, and Christ had shaped his image and understanding of God.

• Jackie experienced God as a presence always with her (sometimes behind her left shoulder) and in all people and groups, and Jesus as in a mediating function with God and of God.

Advances in Readiness

Question fifteen on the intake questionnaire asked the respondent to "place a check mark beside any of the following issues in your readiness for ministry in which you perceive that you need to gain more clarity," and then presented a choice of nine issues. The following is an accounting of which categories in question fifteen each student designated at intake time as personal issues. It also indicates how much if any progress the student perceived was made in each issue by termination time, as the student used the termination questionnaire.

Question fifteen: issues of readiness

    a. Conviction of a call by God to ministry

        Jim--clear progress
        Jackie--clear progress

    b. A sense of your specific form of ministry

        Elizabeth--mixed progress

Kathy--mixed progress
Jim--clear progress
Jackie--clear progress

c. Concern for, and ability to relate openly
    with, other people, especially in reference to
    their Christian faith and living

    Kathy--mixed progress
    Jackie--clear progress

d. Strength of your Christian faith for
    proclaiming the gospel to others

    Elizabeth--clear progress
    Jackie--clear progress

e. Awareness of God's active presence in the
    world

    Jim--mixed progress

f. Personal experience of an ongoing relationship
    with God that affects personal outlook and
    conduct

    Elizabeth--clear progress
    Jackie--clear progress

g. Ability to recognize how the Bible (especially
    the life and ministry of Jesus) addresses your
    own life and the lives of other persons and
    groups

    Kathy--no progress

h. Pursuing a disciplined prayer and worship life
    that provides personal nourishment for minis-
    try with others

    Elizabeth--clear progress
    Kathy--clear progress
    Jim--clear progress
    Jackie--clear progress

i. Recognition of gifts you possess that are
    required for your ministry

    Elizabeth—clear progress
    Kathy—clear progress

    It is notable that the only categories checked by
more than two participants were b. and h., which were
unanimously found to be germane. They were selected
by the students as issues "in which you perceive that
you need to gain more clarity." The unanimity
remains intact if we add the two other seminarians to
whom I administered the questionnaires, a man whom I
saw ten times and a woman whom I saw fourteen times.
Even though each one of the six started seminary with
some degree of conviction about being intended for a
form of ministry, it was a cause of concern and sometimes anxiety to discover more precisely what God
intended. Not only their careers but also their
sense of purpose, value and integrity depended on it.
    All of them believed they would be most likely to
discover the needed revelation through a disciplined
prayer and worship life. Much as they valued the
intellectual training they were receiving in their
courses, they found that this training generally had
only an occasional and secondary impact on their
needs for guidance and prayer. Field education had
more impact for some. Even though all of the seminarians had been unfamiliar with spiritual direction
until our work together, they all looked with greatest hope to spiritual direction to help them with
these specific concerns, as well as the broader ones
about communication with God.
    Did spiritual direction help these students to be
more prepared to serve others in ministries? Each of
the four studied witnessed that it did, based on the
development of a deeper relationship with God and on
progress in the criteria of readiness, as indicated
earlier in this chapter and in the previous chapter.
Of the twenty termination responses regarding the
issues listed under question fifteen, there were
fifteen "clear progress," four "mixed progress," and
only one "no progress." Each student separately
observed that the learnings and maturing of faith
gained through this one-to-one process provided an

indispensable complement without which academic
scholarship would have been frustratingly inadequate.

Similar evidence was added by other seminarians
with whom I worked. The other man who answered the
questionnaires, a twenty-three-year-old junior prepar-
ing for parish ministry in the United Church of
Christ, with whom I met ten times beginning in
February, wrote at the end:

> "Awareness of God's active presence in the world"
> has been the big breakthrough!. . .(During Lent)
> it was simply so obvious that the Holy Spirit was
> working and moving that coincidence no longer had
> a place in my life. . . . I'm more sensitive in
> my personal outlook to what God may be trying to
> say. . . . As my spiritual disciplines lead me
> deeper and help clarify my Christian faith it
> actually becomes a more sensitive area to deal
> with and share. . . . I recognize that I cannot
> function in ministry without worship and prayer,
> (which) provide my nourishment and greatly affect
> my strength to work with others. . . . Spiritual
> direction has made me concerned and quite aware of
> the faith of others and it has given me a real
> desire to work with people on that level.

The other remaining questionnaire respondent was a
divorced Unitarian Universalist woman of forty-six,
in her third year of a five-year M.Div. program, whom
I saw fourteen times starting in December. She began
by saying that what she was seeking through spiritual
direction was "to find the time to establish a prayerful relationship with what I consider God to be."
Her preferred word for the divine was "Spirit," which
she thought of as within people. "Right now," she
wrote, "God is love and the positive forces in the
world. I think God is an interior concept of
wo/man's. This image will grow in time." She followed a practice of reading briefly every morning in
a book of guidance, but seldom prayed. She had
little notion of the type of ministry that might be
right for her. By May, her prayers were very brief
and tentative but also were daily. Toward the end,
she was observing an evening as well as a morning
prayer period. She said:

Getting me to pray was a big step. I've
discovered that daily practice is important, and
the value increases. The ritual aspect is important, too, praying whether I feel like it or not.
Prayer, together with spiritual direction, has
been strengthening my faith, although I sure wish
it could go faster. It has also brought me to the
point where I can almost say that I have a call by
Spirit to ministry, which I couldn't say last
fall. My recent realization that I might be able
to work as a counselor has given new spirit to my
life. I've been able to convey to the people I've
been counseling how important it is to have
faith. My inferior self-image that persisted for
thirteen years has been dissolved with a bang as
I've come to believe I can do this work. This
year's spiritual direction has been an important
beginning. I'm feeling expectant as I anticipate
continuing this work next year, hopefully trying
it with a woman, to help the gains become more
real for me.

It is worthwhile to include the experience of one
other Protestant seminarian, a married woman senior
in her twenties with whom I met for twenty-one times
in the year preceding my formal research project.
Her evaluation at our termination period was another
affirmation of the same themes:

This has been really valuable. Spiritual direction has made a connection of my scholarly world
with my personal world, all related in God's real
presence. Too, it has put the issue of suffering
(which someone brings up weekly in my parish
calling) in a spiritual framework as well as a
colder theological framework. I've learned more
practical theology, in ways that I can use it,
than I did in my seminary courses. Unlike last
September, now I'm able to see myself in a new
identity, more comfortable to be someone with a
personal piety, and identity as a person of the
Bible. Now I relate with the Bible as in dialogue
with the Word of God, different from exegesis.
When I'm ministering to others in my church, I
teach the Bible from my own experience of it.

My own assessment is very strongly supportive of
the students´ views that I have quoted. Even when we
take into account some desire on my part to see my
hypothesis justified, and a possible desire on the
part of some of the participants to be polite or
supportive of my efforts with them, the evidence of
actual happenings in the lives of these people stands
solidly. The fact that there is such a distinctively
individual movement and countermovement from one
person to the next demonstrates that we have been
observers of the authentic, independent struggles and
findings of yearning spiritual travelers who were in
communication with the yearning God.

It further substantiates that, beyond encouraging
the directee to trust God, to make repeated untram-
meled expression to God and to be expectantly and
patiently alert to God´s reply, it is the director´s
place to provide disinterested, prayerful reflection
of the companion´s articulations, as a way of being
God´s agent in evoking the fullest communication that
can be realized between the directee and God. Elizabeth used a graphic analogy when she named my function that of midwife.

Striking Features

The following are eight themes that stood out in the
progress of the students over their months of spiritual direction in preparation for ministry.

1. Integrating

All of the seminarians came with a concern to
attempt, through spiritual direction, to relate their
communicating with God to their academic studies, to
their personal identities, to their potential church
ministries, and to their societal efforts toward
justice and harmony. Jackie articulated the findings
of some, in saying that the combination of academic
study, prayer and spiritual direction was serving her
purpose well. Kathy, starting out and continuing on
a similar search without any anti-intellectualism,
found more trouble with attitudes of both faculty and
fellow students. Thus, at the end of the school

year, she still felt, "I sense a hostility in my world that threatens to wither my faith with logic or ridicule."

2. Praying

Each of the students, concluding that a practice of regular prayer would be indispensable to preparation for a church profession, experimented to find the most fruitful individual rhythm and style. Jim established the most predictable daily practice, including chanting, centering prayer and Scripture meditation. Elizabeth's and Jackie's disciplines combined daily consciousness of God with more free-form utilization of the resources of prayer, dreams, images, writing and intuitions. Kathy moved from sporadic to nearly daily prayers, yet intentionally kept her observances somewhat undisciplined to avoid rigidity or automation.

3. Experiencing God

Direct communication with God became real for Elizabeth, first in her previous conversion experience, and later in a journal message, Scripture, and in the drawing toward ministry as "the unfolding of myself before God." Kathy had known the "reassurance of the presence of God" when she was "almost literally mad with terror" in college. She became convinced that, as she started with Isaiah, she found God calling her by name and was shown the image of the archangel Michael and the half-drowned woman. There was a period in which she was regularly observing evidence of God and receiving guidances, which intensified when the committee rejected her. Jim discovered God in imaginative letter writing, nature, prayer and personal events, heard Jesus address him after reading of the Word, and became aware of a Companion on his pilgrimage toward home. He was given assurance of his being accepted and restored in Jesus Christ, and could state that "a sense of calling to ordained ministry has been clearly given." Jackie was granted revelations through dreams, journal dialogues with Jesus and feeling His touch on her head, through the regal woman and Aunt Kate and the Christ woman in the box.

4. Seeing God's Movements

All of the seminarians became aware of the blessings of being able sometimes to identify specifically what God was doing, in their personal lives and in the larger world's affairs. Elizabeth noticed that God led her to encounter just the people she needed to see at the right times, and that God spoke to her through those others. For example, it was through God's guiding her into spiritual direction that she was able to affirm the value of her own femaleness. Kathy, similarly, recognized God's hand in guiding her to seminary and finding her small support group of fellow-seminarians, and saw that it was even at work in her distressing college infatuation. It became clear to Jim that his initially suspect, "absurd" God had actually been accompanying him all along, guiding and enabling him in the direction of seminary and parish ministry. Through her varied explorations, it became evident to Jackie that divine providence was active in resolving her love affair conflict through self-understanding, enabling her to lead her class in community building, and in all of the small and large circumstances that attracted her to ministerial training and gradually showed her vocational direction. All of the directees found themselves moved toward fuller commitment to involvement in ministries of reconciliation for alleviation of regional and world-scale social inequities, destructiveness and suffering.

5. Feeling

Every participant discovered that the honest and open expression of feelings to God was very facilitating of two-way communication with God. After her reticence about speaking out began to erode, Elizabeth discovered that God was feeling her suffering and wanted a more intimate relationship with her. Kathy recognized it was when she felt devastated by her college infatuation and her rejection by the district committee, after presenting herself arrogantly, when she could no longer hold back her crying out to God, that a transforming awareness of God's presence was given. Jim's experimentation taught

him that dialogic prayer, much more than centering
prayer, connected him consciously with God's movements. Through writing candidly in a journal about
his despair and hopelessness he cleared the way to
receive God's affirmation of His call to ordained
ministry. Jackie was the most constantly and immediately in touch with her feelings. Hence, when she
frankly verbalized to God her skeptical "Is this
mindless dependence, passive femininity?" God was
able to get through with a clear reply, "Jackie, you
are strong enough to be weak now. . . ." It happened
again when she defined and expressed a very specific
need to know the whole God, after she had been split-
ting both God and herself. All four of the students
experienced that God's disclosures through honest
contemplative prayer frequently were attended by
surprises.

6. Growing in Faith

    Not only did faith surge to fuller strength, but
also the ability to articulate faith without embarrassment grew in three of the four student directees.
Hence, Elizabeth stated that "Spiritual Direction has
helped me to be more comfortable with my faith language." The change for Kathy was partial: "My
relationship with God feels quite warm and direct,
and occupies a place of central importance, but I
find it hard to express, and feel a need to protect
my experiences of God from others." Jim came to feel
more secure in talking with both Meg and me about
spiritual experience, as long as he avoided pietistic
language. Jackie felt elated after she realized that
she had rather spontaneously given a clear witness
for her Christian faith in a sermon, and that it had
seemed authentic. She wrote that our process had
"helped me gain a feeling of integrity with my use of
Christian faith."

7. Relating with Others

    The students had not anticipated that they would
receive the benefit of improved relationships with
other people through spiritual direction. Yet all of
them gladly took note of, and welcomed this bonus,
particularly since it also involved more sound

self-confidence and faith-confidence. As tenacious
guilt gradually yielded to faith and self-esteem in
Elizabeth, she began to notice how her relationships
with other people were intertwined with her relationship with God, and her opportunities to love expanded. She mentioned "freedom for myself by which
and through which I can invite others to the Good
News." As Kathy moved beyond fear and self-rejection
and blaming God, she found reconciliation with
parents, grandmother, ex-boyfriend, feminists,
professors, seminary and church. She wrote "I am
learning how to take seriously the command to love
both enemies and neighbors as self." Jim observed,
"At times I am aware of a greater sense of peace and
openness to others growing out of this relationship
with God." Jackie increased in her ability to be
accepting of a critical professor, a male friend, and
one particularly pugnacious campus feminist. All
recognized that the improvements in their abilities
to relate with others would prove pivotal in ministry.

8. Resisting

A particularly striking feature that sometimes
became prominent with all of the students was that of
resisting the very intimacy with God that they
craved. They were generally surprised when they saw
this countermovement in themselves, and sometimes
horrified. Yet they often found it amazingly persis-
tent. In some instances a person tended to confuse
troubled feelings toward an annoying person or the
fallible seminary or church with feelings toward
God. There was almost always some muddying of the
waters by childhood conditioning, notably in the
cases of Jim and Jackie. The basic core of resistance lay in conflict of wills: the anxiety that, if
God came recognizably close, God´s desires would
become evident and might present unwelcome demands
for change, together with guilt about the avoidance.
Elizabeth, avoiding contemplative encounter with
God, early penetrated the dynamic with her admis-
sion: "I feel afraid to get intimate with God, lest
God put a demand on me to sacrifice too much, even to
become a martyr. . . .lose my personal identity."

In a later session, when she was struggling with multiple needs and yet was avoiding God, she put it: "I'm not sure if I want to ask. It seems kinda scary. God might ask something of me that I'm not ready to give." Elizabeth came to this beautiful insight and resolution in our next meeting:

I realize that I've been intentionally choosing anxiety-death-intellect rather than trust-life-heart. I see, too, what advantages there supposedly were in holding onto my anxiety, along with trying-working-proving-controlling.

Kathy, too, was able to concede, "I'm afraid I might receive a different response than I want." She added the additional reason for avoidance, that praying often brought her hurts up to consciousness. Then she was able to give assent that God's seeming absence was tied in with her estrangement from Peter. Her antagonism against the church and school was another thread in the same fabric in her "tough, tough year."

When Jim observed that he failed to follow through on asking God directly about God's nature and his own sexual nature, and then that he was quick to raise obstacles that might prevent him from qualification for ministry, it came as no surprise. After all, part of his mind kept insisting that it was absurd to think that God even existed. There was a particularly keen insight in his pinpointing, "I think that to admit that I had received something from God would feel as though I were giving in to what I had chosen not to be in my identity."

Jackie was another one who was honest enough with herself and me to confess that getting closer to God would be accompanied by the risk of possibly being led where she would not choose to go. It seemed likely that this fear fed her initial reluctance to ask God to speak to her through Scripture passages. And she, like Jim, carried an investment in a previous choice of identity, so that she was determined to avoid "mindless dependency, passive femininity" even in relationship with God, and particularly with the male Master Jesus. Also like Jim, part of her holding back had to do with her resolve not to become entangled with the nonexistent God of her inherited childhood image.

We need to understand the countermovement in these instances with all four students as an acceptable and typical characteristic of spiritual journeyers. It will be worth our lingering just briefly on this dynamic in order to be as clear as possible about it.

When the man in Eden heard the Lord God calling, he replied, "I heard the sound of thee in the garden, and I was afraid, because I was naked; and I hid myself." The people of Israel stood trembling at the base of Sinai, and said to Moses, "You speak to us and we will hear; but let not God speak to us, lest we die." When the word of the Lord directed Jonah to undertake a mission to the people of Nineveh, "Jonah rose to flee to Tarshish from the presence of the Lord." When Simon Peter saw a net-breaking catch of fish hauled in, in response to Jesus' direction, "he fell down at Jesus' knees, saying, 'Depart from me, for I am a sinful man, O Lord.'"[1] Countermovement was boldly evident in Jesus' first apostles when Jesus violated their preconceptions about Him by warning them of His coming suffering and death.

Barry and Connolly provide this helpful explanation:

> Relationships do not develop smoothly. There is something in us that resists change and development, that wants wives or husbands, friends, companions to be the same tomorrow as they are today. At the same time, there is something in us that wants to know more about the other and is bored by sameness. These two desires clash in us and produce conflict and resistance. Resistance is a critical element in the development of every interpersonal relationship. It does, therefore, play a part in the development of a relationship with God.[2]

Frans Jozef van Beeck offers this complementary interpretation:

> But as a matter of actual fact, rather than accepting the strangeness of the other--whether God, person, or thing--as a gracious invitation, we tend to be threatened by it, to keep it at arm's length, to protect ourselves against it, to sit in judgment on it, to drag it before the

tribunal of our ego, to measure it by the standard of our discernments, and to overpower it. In the light of this defensive attitude, the direct act of encounter starts to look like an undesirable thing to do; the available experience of graciousness starts to appear as the enemy of established nature.[3]

No wonder so many of us recognize a truth about ourselves in Francis Thompson's echoing poetry:

I fled Him, down the nights and down the days;
  I fled Him, down the arches of the years;
I fled Him, down the labyrinthine ways
  Of my own mind; and in the midst of tears
I hid from Him, and under running laughter. . . .
(For, though I knew His love Who followed,
  Yet was I sore adread
Lest, having Him, I must have naught beside)
. . . .[4]

It was repeatedly a cause for rejoicing for me that, when a directee did eventually feel ready to risk encounter with the mysterium tremendum, she or he before long felt not only relieved but also very satisfied and gratified at having ventured the initiative. Actually, what seemed like a directee's initiative generally came to be acknowledged as a response. The constantly repeated experience was that, consistent with the revelation in Jesus' earthly ministry, God turned out to be far less harsh and threatening than has been feared. It was the Almighty who had all the time been patiently yearning in love for more closeness and mutual acceptance.

The eighth feature, of countermovement, may not seem at first to have directly advanced the students' readiness for ministry. Their experience of it surely did so indirectly, however. They were distinctly more prepared by virtue of knowing themselves more honestly than before and of understanding more realistically what is entailed in getting close to God. To that extent they were rendered more able to guide people in their future ministries who will undertake similar journeys.

Three capital findings stand out from reflection in the eight striking features just described. The firsthand experience of the students demonstrates that: 1) God is urgently ready to open the door of dialogue and assistance to anyone who is unreservedly earnest in approaching; 2) it is astoundingly typical, even of hungry seekers, to hold tenaciously to certain specific boundaries beyond which they resist God's advances; and, 3) God will not violate a person's limits and dignity, however powerful the divine longing of love, but will wait for mutual readiness. It is critical that as many as possible enter ministries knowing these truths from their own experiences as well as the descriptions of others.

Conclusions

Although the empirical data are limited to the results of research with a few students, I believe that they indicate substantiation of the hypothesis set forth in Chapter II, that spiritual direction has the potential of being a strong force in advancing Protestant seminarians in their readiness for ministry.

If I were to do the project over again, I would consider including these additional criteria for measuring progress:

● Ability to be in touch with feelings, to identify and express them appropriately

● Deepening acceptance and love of self, others and God

● Allowing God the freedom to be God

● Creativity and imagination, humor and freedom of spirit, as characteristics of ministerial style

● Courage to take stands for convictions, in religious and secular communities, even in the face of opposition

My observation of the students in the course of my project alerted me to see that these factors are significant in personal life and in public ministry. They are worthy to be singled out for attention.

It is my conviction and that of the students that even these few months of spiritual direction supplemented their course work and field education with a crucially important component that was unavailable to them through any other avenue. What could be more important to these ministers-in-formation than to have encountered God repeatedly in direct and partially describably ways, together with studying about other people's descriptions of the divine? The ring of authenticity and confidence in their witness to the faith cannot help but be truer as a result of their having had the gospel happen to them first-hand. It is also part of my hypothesis that a substantial proportion of students throughout seminaries would benefit vastly if spiritual direction were made available to them and they availed themselves of it.

It was Jim's judgment that, in dealing with the multiple training factors such as courses, conversations with others and field education, "the effect of the spiritual direction experience has been to make me more attentive to those 'other factors.'" I covet this profit as an opportunity for all seminarians everywhere.

It is important to me to add that the features I have described as observed in the spiritual direction process with the four students are in no way peculiar to seminarians. On the contrary, they are widely representative of other Christians with whom I have worked in similar relationships. The majority of people with whom I have been formally engaged as a spiritual companion have not been seminary students. A few have been engaged in specifically religious vocations: minister, Christian educator, counselor, church staff coordinator, monastic priest, sister, monastery novice. Most, however, have included men and women conscious of engaging in lay Christian ministry while pursuing careers of a wide variety: homemaker and parent, community volunteer, secretary, social worker, teacher, nurse, physicist, meteorologist, physician, writer, editor, organizational development consultant, and others.

My experiences with these—and experiences reported by my colleagues in spiritual guidance—repeatedly confirm that the movements I have described between the directees and the God they have approached with the aid of a trained soul comrade have been considerably characterized by the descriptions I have given above. I conclude that spiritual direction is a remarkably effective process for enhancing readiness for ministry on the part of a broad spectrum of Christian disciples.

One evidence of this effectiveness came in the form of a note I received from a former directee. In the months since I had moved from her area, she had suffered from a broken engagement and disruption in her employment. She wrote:

Were it not for the knowledge that God is there prodding, providing, coaxing me into growth, I would lose strength. But after my counseling with you, Forster, I can see the richness of the time ahead and can feel grateful to God for prodding and forcing me (because I'd never do it on my own) and leaving me no choice but to accept it and grow. You may remember, I didn't have any faith before, and now I do and it makes all the difference.

Recommendations

Broad vistas of God's possibilities lie before us, beckoning us to explore and discover. What a few have been learning about the wonders of spirituality surely are about to be expanded by others through further research. Like the descendants of Abraham and Sarah, the promises to the people God loves are "as many as the stars of heaven and as the innumerable grains of sand by the seashore."[5]

A pastor contacted me who said that he had become so discouraged with his career that he had tried to quit the ministry. He had given most of his books to a library, but the library returned them. He had applied for other kinds of jobs and was offered two on the same day, then knew that his calling was in the church and there must be some way to prepare himself so he could stay in it with equanimity.

He had seen himself as an able intellectual; he felt afraid of pursuing prayer and giving over control to God. In recent months, however, he had felt a yearning for something more spiritual, developed largely through his struggles in ministry, demonstrations of his wife's faith, his dreams, prayers, journal, Scripture and participating in a workshop series that I offered. He had been unaware until just recently that spiritual direction was available, or where it was available. Now he could see that what would help him most would be guidance with prayer, to develop a more open relationship with God. He was convinced that this would add the most to his effectiveness and satisfaction in ministry.

Numerous other church professionals have confessed to me with embarrassment that they have no devotional life worthy of the name and that no one ever taught them how to pray. It is clear to me that these are representative of a host of others.

The church has no need and no right to permit such sad and hypocritical conditions to persist among their supposed spiritual leaders. An increasing number of these people feel very earnest about wanting to learn how to function effectively in the spiritual realm, and there are countless congregations that would be excited to support them in seeking such learning if the leaders dared to confess their need and if they knew where to seek.

I fully concur with the conclusion,

Probably for only a very few especially "graced" persons can such progress be made alone, without help from more spiritually developed persons. We believe that it is the primary job of authentic religious institutions to help individuals (and whole communities and societies, if possible) to make such progress. To enhance this helping capacity should be the primary job of future research in this area.[6]

Our seminaries are the arm of the church that holds the strongest potential for righting our imbalance and for building foundational strength into ministry in the years immediately ahead. There is no need for them to fear that the more intentional pursuit of spirituality will make their present efforts

appear insignificant. On the contrary, the spiritual, academic and practical belong together for
mutual support and affirmation of meaning. Simone
Weil articulates this reality:

> The key to a Christian conception of studies is
> the realization that prayer consists of atten-
> tion. It is the orientation of all the attention
> of which the soul is capable toward God. The
> quality of the attention counts for much in the
> quality of the prayer. Warmth of heart cannot
> make up for it. . . .
>
> It is the part played by joy in our studies that
> makes of them a preparation for spiritual life,
> for desire directed toward God is the only power
> capable of raising the soul. Or rather, it is God
> alone who comes down and possesses the soul, but
> desire alone draws God down. He only comes to
> those who ask him to come; and he cannot refuse to
> come to those who implore him long, often, and
> ardently.[7]

The development of spiritual vitality in students is
the most natural fulcrum to balance and integrate the
various pressuring components of preparation for ministry which currently produce tumult in many.

    I consequently make the following recommenda-
tions. These recommendations are built on the
assumption that the school already has an adequate or
developing offering of various experiences in corpor-
ate worship as an indispensable common foundation for
all members of its community. Such experiences most
likely should range from small student-led Bible-
prayer-support groups, through faculty-assisted
explorations into spiritual disciplines with faith
sharing, and perhaps morning, noon and evening prayer
opportunities, to at least weekly all-community cele-
bration of Word and Sacrament.

1. Each Protestant seminary administration, in consul-
tation with faculty members and students, should
obtain the services of a trained spiritual formation

team. It should then make known to the students what spiritual direction is, what its benefits might be and how to avail themselves of it, and should encourage them to try a series of exploratory meetings. Introduction by way of experiential courses in spiritual disciplines for ministry, or spiritual search groups, would be appropriate in many cases. These should be backed up by enriching present and evolving curricula with attention to the history, theology, phenomenology, psychology and practice of Christian spirituality, and by off-campus overnight retreats (not seminars) perhaps three times a year. The seminary should make personal and group guidance available to its staff and faculty members as well as its students.

2. Establishing such a team can begin with a single individual, even on a part-time basis. Ideally, such a person should be considered staff rather than a faculty member, or at least should not work with individual directees who would also be enrolled in graded courses s/he teaches. It would be suitable for the spiritual direction function to be performed by someone in the position of chaplain or pastor to the seminary. Minimally, students could be referred to one or more qualified Christian guides in the geographical vicinity.

3. A seminary will need to consider, as a next step after providing spiritual direction, offering training to more experienced M.Div., graduate and continuing education students in the history, theory and practice of spiritual direction, as some schools have already begun to do. This will be essential in order for our tradition to build up a body of well-qualified practitioners in this field, for parishes, judicatories, chaplaincies and other ministerial settings. There are already several Protestant seminaries and institutes in the United States that offer certificate or degree programs in spiritual direction, in addition to a few Roman Catholic programs. These courses of study take their bearings from a variety of orientations, such as Ignatian, Jungian, eastern religions and church organization leadership.

4. It will be important for members of spiritual formation staffs of seminaries and institutes to continue researching and reporting on their findings in this revivified discipline. There is need for them also to take responsibility to offer consultations and publications to keep other church leaders informed of progress.

5. Each church judicatory and religious order should inform itself about, and take maximum advantage of, spiritual direction and related methods of personal care and formation for the benefit of its professional and lay constituents. For a beginning, certified spiritual guides could well be employed for positions already in place, such as director of religious life, orientation coordinator for seminary graduates in their first five years, or pastor to clergy and their families. Judicatory personnel in such posts commonly deal with clergy and lay people feeling vulnerable and receptive to deeper resources. It will be wise at the same time to foster the multiplication of now rare specialized parish staff positions in spiritual direction and training.

6. Creative means of financing will be found. Although church organizations and especially seminaries are widely feeling monetarily besieged, God can be trusted to open the way to a goal that God designs and disciples of Christ desire. As people are becoming more conscious that direct communication with God is readily available, and their longing to experience it heightens, we can expect that certain individuals with vision will be successfully challenged to provide funding for new spiritual expeditions who have not been motivated to fund other seminary programs. Their gifts will extend what some farsighted foundations have already been beginning.

One reason why people are intensifying their spiritual searching is that they experience their world as alarmingly tortured and feel pressed to find a path to a harmonious stewardship. The major reason why we become more engaged in the depths of God´s redeeming nature, which is supremely revealed and accessible in Jesus Christ, is that this is the human pursuit that holds the most promise of bringing

healing, justice and peace to God´s creation. This
can help open the way to manifestation that God´s "is
the kingdom and the power and the glory, forever."[8]

APPENDIX

The following was administered to all of the students
early in our sessions together, with appropriate
spaces included for their responses.

Spiritual Direction Intake Questionnaire

Date_____

1. Name

2. Seminary, intended degree and year of graduation

3. Single, married, divorced, remarried

4. Age

5. Denomination

6. Vocational goal

7. How much experience have you had previously with
   a spiritual director, if any?

8. What are you seeking through spiritual direction?

9. What are you hoping not to find (what might
   alienate you)?

10. Do you have an image(s) of what God is like for
    you? If so, please describe.

11. What part, if any, does Jesus Christ have in your
    relationship with God?

12. What is your most memorable spiritual experience, if any?

13. What problems, if any, do you have about your relationship with God?

14. What spiritual practices, if any, do you have now?

15. Please place a check mark beside any of the following issues in your readiness for ministry in which you perceive that you need to gain more clarity:

   a. Conviction of a call by God to ministry
   b. A sense of your specific form of ministry
   c. Concern for, and ability to relate openly with, other people, especially in reference to their Christian faith and living
   d. Strength of your Christian faith for proclaiming the gospel to others
   e. Awareness of God's active presence in the world
   f. Personal experience of an ongoing relationship with God that affects personal outlook and conduct
   g. Ability to recognize how the Bible (especially the life and ministry of Jesus) addresses your own life and the lives of other persons and groups
   h. Pursuing a disciplined prayer and worship life that provides personal nourishment for ministry with others
   i. Recognition of gifts you possess that are required for your ministry
   j. Other

16. Any further comments that you want to add

   The framing of this Intake Questionnaire was revised for use at termination. I deleted questions 2-7 and 10 and revised 8 and 9 to read, "What have you lately been. . .?" The original question 15 was revised to read, "Please describe what differences, if any, you perceive that your experience in spiritual direction has made in your readiness for ministry in the following areas: . . . ."

NOTES

PREFACE

1. Experiencing the Depths of Jesus Christ,
Library of Christian Classics, II (Goleta, CA:
Christian Books, 1975), pp. x-xi.

CHAPTER 1:

1. Based on Ephrem Carr, OSB, "The History of
Spiritual Direction," lectures given as part of a
course, "Doing Spiritual Direction in a Protestant
Context," St. Meinrad School of Theology, June 13-17,
1983. Also Kenneth Leech, Soul Friend: The Practice
of Christian Spirituality (San Francisco: Harper &
Row, 1977), Chapters 2, 4.
  2. 1 Samuel 3:1 (RSV).
  3. Mark 12:29-30 (RSV).
  4. Olen B. Landes, "Dangerous Trends in the
Church Today," Pulpit Helps, September 1979, p. 1.
  5. Tilden H. Edwards, Jr. et al., Spiritual
Growth: An Empirical Exploration of its Meaning,
Sources and Implications (Washington: Metropolitan
Ecumenical Training Center, Inc., 1974), pp. 9-10.
  6. "The Future of Education for the Ministry,"
Haelen, Spring and Fall 1982, p. 25.
  7. Roy M. Oswald, Crossing the Boundary Between
Seminary and Parish (Washington, DC: The Alban
Institute, Inc., 1980), p. 13.
  8. Ibid., p. 18.
  9. Tilden H. Edwards, Jr., "Spiritual Formation
in Theological Schools," Theological Education,
Autumn 1980, p. 21.
  10. David S. Schuller et al., Readiness for
Ministry, II (Vandalia, OH: Association of
Theological Schools in the United States and Canada,
1976), pp. 9, 13.
  11. Jean Houston´s term.

12. Carnegie Samuel Calian, "Is the Seminary a Church?", The Christian Century, Feb. 2-9, 1983, p. 118.

13. Hugh Anderson, "A Few Reflections on Theological Education," New College Bulletin, September, 1980, pp. 4, 11.

14. With the Door Open, trans. Erwin and Pleasaunce von Gaisberg, in The Protestant Mystics, ed. Anne Fremantle (New York: Mentor, 1965), p. 249.

15. David C. Babin et al., Voyage--Vision--Venture (Dayton, OH: American Association of Theological Schools in the United States and Canada, 1972), pp. 8, 9.

16. See n. 9 above, pp. 14, 16.

17. "Theological Education and the New Spirituality," The Presbyterian Outlook, October 23, 1967, pp. 6-7.

18. "The Challenge to the Seminary," Christianity and Crisis, April 14, 1969, pp. 81-83.

19. "Theology and Theopoetic," The Christian Century, May 23, 1973, pp. 593-95.

20. Archie Smith, Jr., "The Meaning of Spirituality in the Preparation for Life: An Empirical Approach," Encounter, August 1979, pp. 380-81.

21. "The President's Report," Union Theological Seminary, 1981, Special Edition, pp. 8-9.

22. Pat McCallum, "Someone to Talk To," survey questionnaire, 1981.

23. Christopher Fry, A Sleep of Prisoners (New York: Oxford, 1951), pp. 47-48.

CHAPTER 2:

1. e.g., Ezekiel 11:19-20; Jeremiah 31:33; Matthew 18:1-4; 22:1-14; 24:36-44; Luke 7:28; 12:35-40; 17:21; John 3:3; 14:12; Romans 12:2; 1 Corinthians 15:51-52; 2 Corinthians 5:17; Galatians 2:20; 6:15; Ephesians 4:11-16, 22-24; Philippians 2:5-8; Colossians 2:12; 3:1-4, 9-11; 1 Timothy 6:12; James 1:16-18; 2 Peter 1:4-11; 1 John 3:2-3; 5:11-12.

2. John 14:12; Romans 12:2; Luke 17:21 (NEB).

3. Schuller (See n. 10, Chapter 1), I, vi.

4. Ibid, I, iv.

5. Ibid, I, 15.

6. Ibid. I, 91-92.

7. William A. Barry and William J. Connolly, The Practice of Spiritual Direction (New York: Seabury, 1982), p. 8.

8. Ibid., p. 46.

9. Glenn Hinson, "The History of Spirituality," lectures on unpublished tape.

10. Comparisons are made in Ruth Tiffany Barnhouse, "Spiritual Direction and Psychotherapy," Journal of Pastoral Care, September 1979; William Barry, "Spiritual Direction and Pastoral Counseling," Pastoral Psychology, Fall, 1977; William J. Connolly, "Contemporary Spiritual Direction: Scope and Principles," Studies in the Spirituality of Jesuits, June 1975; Edwards, "Spiritual Formation"; Roy W. Fairchild, "Guaranteed Not to Shrink: Spiritual Direction in Pastoral Care," Pastoral Psychology, Winter 1982; Fairchild, "The Pastor as Spiritual Director, Quarterly Review, Summer 1985; and Leech, Chapter 3.

11. Edwards (See n. 9, Chapter 1), p. 10.

12. "Spirituality and Going to Seminary (suggestions for seminarians)," Center for Christian Spirituality, General Theological Seminary, pp. 1, 4, 5, 6, 9.

13. Stages of Faith: The Psychology of Human Development and the Quest for Meaning (San Francisco: Harper & Row, 1981), pp. 182-83.

14. "Contemporary Challenges to Issues of Vocational Preparation," Theological Education, Autumn 1982, pp. 101, 102, 104.

15. Edwards (See n. 9, Chapter 1),pp. 15, 17.

16. Ibid., pp. 23-26.

17. Ibid., Summary of an address, "Excellence of Mind, Excellence of Spirit," pp. 35-36.

18. New Seeds of Contemplation (New York: New Directions, 1962), pp. 254-55.

CHAPTER 3:

1. Psalm 103:1; 139:13-14a (RSV).

CHAPTER 4:

1. Genesis 3:10; Exodus 20:19, Jonah 1:3; Luke 5:8 (RSV).

2. Barry and Connolly (See n. 7, Chapter 2), pp. 80-81.

3. Frans Jozef van Beeck, Christ Proclaimed (New York: Paulist Press, 1979), p. 244.

4. "The Hound of Heaven," in Immortal Poems of the English Language, ed. Oscar Williams (New York: Pocket-Simon & Schuster, 1952), pp. 476-77.

5. Hebrews 11:12 (RSV).

6. Edwards (See n. 5, Chapter 1), p. 50.

7. Waiting for God, trans. Emma Craufurd (New York: G.P. Putnam's Sons, 1951), pp. 105, 110-11.

8. Matthew 6:13 (RSV).

BIBLIOGRAPHY

A. BOOKS

Babin, David E., Lewis A. Briner, Paul W. Hoon,
Robert W. Martin, Jr., Terry Smith, Eugene I. Van
Antwerp, and Paul J. Whitney, Voyage-Vision-
Venture, Dayton: American Association of Theo-
logical Schools, 1972.
Barry, William A. and William J. Connolly, The
Practice of Spiritual Direction, New York:
Seabury Press, 1982.
Dyckman, Katherine Marie and L. Patrick Carroll,
Inviting the Mystic, Supporting the Prophet, New
York: Paulist Press, 1981.
Edwards, Tilden H., Spiritual Friend, New York:
Paulist Press, 1980.
Edwards, Tilden H., Loren B. Mead, Parker J. Palmer,
James P. Simmons, Spiritual Growth: An Empirical
Exploration of its Meaning, Sources and Implica-
tions, Washington, DC: Metropolitan Ecumenical
Training Center, 1974.
Fleming, David L., S.J., ed., Notes on the Spiritual
Exercises of St. Ignatius of Loyola, St. Louis:
Review for Religious, 1981.
-----, The Spiritual Exercises of St. Ignatius: A
Literal Translation and a Contemporary Reading,
St. Louis: Institute of Jesuit Sources, 1978.
Fletcher, John C., The Futures of Protestant
Seminaries, Washington, DC: The Alban Institute,
1983.
Fowler, James W., Stages of Faith, San Francisco:
Harper & Row, 1981.
Leech, Kenneth, Soul Friend: The Practice of
Christian Spirituality, San Francisco: Harper &
Row, 1977.
May, Gerald G., Pilgrimage Home, New York: Paulist
Press, 1979.
Olin, John C., ed., The Autobiography of St. Ignatius
Loyola, New York: Torchbooks, Harper & Row, 1974.

Oswald, Roy M., Crossing the Boundary between Seminary and Parish, Washington, DC: The Alban Institute, 1980.

Palmer, Parker J., To Know as We Are Known, San Francisco: Harper & Row, 1983.

Schuller, David S., Milo L. Brekke, Merton P. Strommen, Daniel O. Aleshire, Readiness for Ministry, Vols. I and II, Vandalia, Ohio: Association of Theological Schools, 1975, 1976.

Van Beeck, Frans Jozef, S.J., Christ Proclaimed: Christology as Rhetoric, New York: Paulist Press, 1979.

Weil, Simone, Waiting for God, New York: G.P. Putnam's Sons, 1951.

B. ARTICLES AND TAPES

Ashmall, Donald H., "Spiritual Development and the Free Church Tradition," Andover Newton Quarterly, January, 1980.

Barnhouse, Ruth Tiffany, "Spiritual Direction and Psychotherapy," Journal of Pastoral Care, September, 1979.

Barry, William A., "Contemplative Prayer and the Study of Theology," Theology Digest, Summer, 1976.

-----, "Spiritual Direction and Pastoral Counseling," Pastoral Psychology, Fall, 1977.

Casey, Noah, "Group Faith-Sharing and Individual Spiritual Direction in a College Seminary," Weston D.Min. thesis, 1981.

Connolly, William J., "Contemporary Spiritual Direction: Scope and Principles," Studies in the Spirituality of Jesuits, June 1975.

-----, "Spiritual Direction: It Begins with Experience," Human Development, Spring, 1980.

Connolly, William, S.J., Madeline Birmingham, r.c. and Anne Harvey, S.N.D., Prayer as Dialogue, 3 cassette tapes, LC 47, Cleveland: Audio Communications Center.

Connolly, Bill, S.J., William Barry, S.J., Anne Harvey, S.N.D. and Paul Lucey, S.J., Initiating Spiritual Direction, 3 cassette tapes, Cleveland: Audio Communications Center.

Cunningham, Fred B., "A Presbytery Program of Spiritual Formation for Candidates for the Ministry," Louisville D.Min. thesis, 1982.

Edwards, Tilden H., Jr., "Spiritual Formation in
    Theological Schools: Ferment and Challenge,"
    Theological Education, Autumn, 1980.
Fairchild, Roy W., "Guaranteed Not to Shrink:
    Spiritual Direction in Pastoral Care," Pastoral
    Psychology, Winter, 1982.
Howe, Reuel, "The Future of Education for Ministry,"
    Haelen, Spring and Fall, 1982.
Jones, Alan, "Spirituality and Going to Seminary,"
    "What Happens in Spiritual Direction?", General
    Theological Seminary.
Jones, W. Paul, cons. ed., "Focus on the Pastor and
    Spiritual Formation," Quarterly Review, Summer,
    1985.
McCallum, Pat, "Someone to Talk To," Survey of
    Andover Newton Theological School student
    community by the Andover Newton Women's Caucus,
    1981.
Parks, Sharon, "Contemporary Challenges to Issues of
    Vocational Preparation," Theological Education,
    Autumn, 1982.
Smith, Archie, "The Meaning of Spirituality in the
    Preparation for Life: An Empirical Approach,"
    Encounter, August, 1979.

You may also be interested in these
Alban Institute publications. . .

<u>Crossing the Boundary Between Seminary and Parish</u>, by
Roy M. Oswald. A study of clergy in transition
revealed that most clergy experienced great difficul-
ties in moving from seminaries into their first
full-time parish ministries. This compilation of
research results sheds light on the culture shock,
the areas of competence and unpreparedness seminary
graduates experience when they start work in their
first parish. (AL43)

<u>A Faith for the Middle Years</u> by Daniel B. Leavitt.
In an analysis of what faith means to middle adults
(40-60 years old), Leavitt incorporates original
research and an overview of the work of writers in
the field of adult development, as well as of
students of faith development. This invaluable aid
to those ministering to people in the mid-life stage
clarifies the differences between the male and female
developmental journey, and the religious pilgrimage
of laity and clergy. (AL59)

<u>Explorations in Faith</u>, Leader´s Guide by Robert A.
Evans, G. Douglass Lewis and Marjorie Hall Davis.
Presented in the context of real-life issues that
puzzle and trouble us all, this six-session course
developed at the Hartford Seminary enables clergy and
laity to share theological resources. Session titles
are: "What is Faith?"; "Meaning"; "Belonging";
"Empowering"; "Acting in the World"; and "Facing
Death". Two educational methods are highlighted:
Bible study with detailed instruction by Walter Wink;
and case studies to provide a real-life context for
the issues. (Leader´s Guide AL58, Participants´
Packet AL58P)

<u>The Futures of Protestant Seminaries</u> by John C.
Fletcher. Here are careful analyses of trends,
programs, challenges and solutions in seminary
education. (AL75)

<u>Ministry as Reflective Practice</u>: a new look at the
professional model by Jackson W. Carroll. Churches
want competent, professional clergy. But the

96

professional model of ministry has received some criticisms that need to be heard. Rather than discarding professionalism, Carroll reconceives it, proposing a view of clergy as "reflective practitioners" who have expertise as meaning definers, as community builders, and as managers of the interface between the church and its social context. (AL89)

New Beginnings: Pastorate Start-Up Workbook by Roy M. Oswald. This notebook will help clergy--in groups or as individuals--work on terminating their previous pastorate, cope with the stress of transition, and enter the new pastorate with a plan for their ministry. (AL32)

Religious Authenticity in the Clergy by John C. Fletcher. The stages of growth between a pastor and congregation are conceptualized in a fresh way. Three crises emerge through which a clergyperson becomes authenticated as minister of a congregation. (AL10)

Stress, Power and Ministry by John C. Harris. A "classic" Alban Institute publication, this handbook for clergy and laity is a result of many years of sensitive work with many churches. Mr. Harris explores the extraordinarily complex, tender creative, and frightening relationship between the work of clergy and the life of laity. The study guide by Jack Harris and Celia Hahn provides designs for 7 two-hour sessions. (AL27, AL27SG)

Women in Parish Ministry: Stress and Support by Marian Coger. United Methodist clergywoman Marian Coger interviewed women pastors in her denomination and an ecumenical group to find out how clergy can take care of themselves so they can avoid burnout, enhance their ministries, get the personal and professional support they need. For clergywomen and clergymen, and also for lay leaders, executives and seminary personnel. (AL87)

Handling charge on each order. Orders under $25 must be prepaid. No postage charged on prepaid orders. Write to The Alban Institute for a complete catalogue of publications.

The Alban Institute:
an invitation to membership

The Alban Institute, begun in 1974, believes that the congregation is essential to the task of equipping the people of God to minister in the church and the world. A multi-denominational membership organization, the Institute provides on-site training, educational programs, consulting, research, and publishing for hundreds of churches across the country.

The Alban Institute invites you to be a member of this partnership of laity, clergy and executives—a partnership that brings together people who are raising important questions about congregational life and people who are trying new solutions, making new discoveries, finding a new way of getting clear about the task of ministry. The Institute exists to provide you with the kinds of information and resources you need to support your ministries.

Join us now and enjoy these benefits:
Publications Discounts:
- 15% for Individual, Contributing and Supporting Members
- 40% for Judicatory and Seminary Executive Members

Discounts on Training and Continuing Education
Action Information, a highly respected journal published 6 times a year, to keep you up to date on current issues and trends.

Write us for more information about how to join The Alban Institute, particularly about Congregational Memberships, in which 10 designated persons (25 for Supporting Congregational Members) receive all benefits of membership.

The Alban Institute, Inc.
4125 Nebraska Avenue, NW
Washington, DC 20016

DATE DUE

JAN 95

FEB 5

AP 97

#LO-45220